Crazy Quilt

Crazy Quilt

By Jocelyn Riley

William Morrow and Company
New York | 1984

The author wishes to acknowledge
the generosity and vision of the
Thomas J. Watson Foundation.

Lyrics and poems by Jocelyn Riley

Printed in the United States of America.

2 3 4 5 6 7 8 9 10

Library of Congress Cataloging in Publication Data
Riley, Jocelyn.   Crazy quilt.
Sequel to: Only my mouth is smiling. Summary: Thirteen-year-old
Merle and her brother and sister return to Chicago to live with their
grandmother and come to terms with the uncertainties caused by their
mother's mental illness. [1. Mentally ill—Fiction. 2. Family problems—
Fiction. 3. Grandmothers—Fiction] I. Title.
PZ7.R454Cr 1984   [Fic]   84-1017
ISBN 0-688-03873-5

To Jeff and Doran

1

"Move it or lose it, Carlson!" someone said. I looked up. Jennifer Normandale—better known as Jinx—was standing in front of me, her hands on her hips.

"What?" I said. "Lose what?"

She laughed. "You are *so* out of it," she said, then turned and tore off down the basketball court after the girl who had the ball.

Good old Jinx Normandale—star of our gym class. Gym was the only class she did well in, and she made sure everyone knew that she was the best in the class. She managed to look good in the stupid gym clothes, even though she wore black tights under the blue shorts and a black, long-sleeved leotard under the short-sleeved white shirt. She didn't care what kind of weird clothes she wore. I was surprised Ms. Garland

1

didn't make her wear the uniform like the rest of us, though.

"I've got it!" Jinx yelled as she ran by again.

"Traveling!" yelled Ms. Garland. Then she blew the silver whistle that hung on a lanyard around her neck.

Jinx kept right on running, then jumped up and tossed the ball through the hoop.

"Didn't you hear me, Jennifer?" the teacher said. "You were traveling. The basket doesn't count."

"I *still* got it," Jinx said. "I don't care if it counts or not." She tossed her head and looked around her. A couple of her friends smiled, and someone whispered, "Atta girl, Jinx."

Jinx looked sideways over toward Ms. Garland. She smiled a sort of jeering smile at her. "A basket's a basket," Jinx said. Someone tossed her the ball, and she caught it, her purple fingernails grasping it like long, hard petals.

"A basket is not a basket," Ms. Garland said. "How can you possibly play a game if you don't follow the rules? A basket counts as a basket only under certain conditions."

"And I suppose *you* get to decide what those conditions are?" Jinx said.

Everybody was looking at her; a lot of girls were sort of half-giggling to themselves. Ms. Garland looked around. "You'd rather make up your own rules, Jennifer? When would you decide that a basket counted, if it were up to you?"

"Whenever *I* made it, it would count," Jinx said. "Simple as that."

Everyone laughed.

"Are you ever going to have a tough row to hoe," Ms. Garland said. "How far do you think you're going to get with attitudes like that?"

"As far as Nancy Lieberman got—that's how far," Jinx said. "Just wait till I'm a star." She tossed her head again, so that her bangs moved over her eyebrows like a soft broom sweeping at the bridge of her nose.

"You think she became a star by mouthing off to her coach?" Ms. Garland asked. "You think she didn't have to learn the rules like everyone else?"

"You're not my coach," Jinx said. She started to dribble the ball.

"Give me that," Ms. Garland said.

Jinx looked off toward the wire-covered clock on the wall and tossed the ball so that it just missed hitting Ms. Garland's hip. The ball rolled off toward the tumbling mats on the wall. "Did you hear me, Jennifer?"

"I can't help it if you're not a very good basketball player," Jinx said. "I don't see how you can be a gym teacher if you can't even catch a basketball."

The entire class sucked in its breath at once. "See me after class," Ms. Garland said. She looked up at the clock. "Hit the showers a little early this morning, girls. There really isn't time to start up again."

But no one moved. We all stood around watching to see what Jinx would do next and sort of rolling our eyes at each other. I mean, how did she dare say things like that to a teacher? Jinx didn't seem to be afraid of anybody.

Ms. Garland picked up her whistle and blew into it three times, short but sharp. Then she dropped the whistle and walked over to her office. She closed the door. Through the glass of the windows, we could see her sit down at her desk and stare over at the pegboard that held all our locker keys. She just sat there, staring, as we all walked slowly toward the showers.

My shower partner was Peggy Conner. Each shower had two changing stalls with a shower stall in the middle. There were curtains on the two outside openings, but the two openings leading into the shower itself had no curtains. So we would undress as close to the curtains as possible, then slink into the shower one at a time.

"You take the first shower, Merle!" Peggy called from her side.

"Okay!" I said. I hurried to take off my clothes and piled them on the tiled wooden bench. I reached in and turned on the water spigot, then stood under it. The water was freezing cold, but as soon as I added more hot, it got too hot. Everyone's shower was the same way, and the whole room was filled with the squeals of girls who were either freezing or scalding.

"I wish she'd hurry," I said to Peggy above the noise of the water.

"Who's in the shower?" the monitor called out. "Carlson or Conner?"

"Carlson!" I said.

"Check," the monitor said, and went on to the next set of showers. Everybody had to take a shower after every gym class. The only way to get out of it was to have your period; then you could go straight from the gym to the locker room and get dressed. Otherwise, it was into the shower you went.

Still, I could have used rules like that—in fact, I could even have used showers like that—when we lived in Lake Lune. That was such a cow town they didn't even have a gym, let alone showers. I guess all the farm kids got their exercise milking cows or something, but for a kid from the suburbs of Chicago, not having gym was strange.

And Bronwyn is the 'burbs. I mean, if you want authentic, genuine, dyed-in-the-wool, 'burb-o-city, just head on out to Bronwyn, Illinois, and you've got it.

On the other hand, if you want an honest-to-God hick town, check out Lake Lune, Wisconsin. I sure didn't know what Mother was getting us into when she dragged us up there. No showers at school were the least of our worries. No hot water at home weighed more on my mind. To say nothing of Mother's weirding out all over the place.

Now I didn't need to take a real shower at school; I could soak clean at home. Grandma's house had plenty of hot water. All I did at school was get wet enough in the shower to get checked off by the monitor.

The minute the monitor checked me off, I jumped out of the shower. "All yours!" I yelled to Peggy.

I dried off, threw on my underwear, and draped a towel around me as I walked out to the locker room for the rest of my clothes. The locker room was empty except for Jinx Normandale, who stood in front of the mirror in black tights and a beige bra. One of her arms was toward me, and I couldn't help staring at it. There was a bruise on her left forearm the size of a grape-fruit. A blackish blue grapefruit with purple red un-dertones. Her skin was dark to begin with, and she still had some of her summer tan left, so the bruise looked really strange and dark.

"What're you staring at, Carlson?" Jinx said when she noticed me. She grabbed her sweater and started to pull it on.

"Oh, um, I didn't mean to stare." I looked quickly down at the floor.

"Why the fuck are you staring then, if you don't mean to?" She jabbed one of her hands into the arm of the sweater.

"I didn't expect anybody to be out here yet," I said. "You don't have to swear at me."

" 'You don't have to swear at me,' " she mimicked in a prissy voice. Her sweater got tangled and she pulled at it. "You riding the rag, or what?"

"Riding the rag?" I knew what it meant, but I didn't want to get into it—least of all with her.

"My, my," she said. "Little Miss Priss is quite the

innocent, isn't she?" As Jinx pulled the sweater over her bruise, she flinched a little.

"Does it hurt?"

"What's it to you? Just shut up, like I said."

I pulled my sweater down over my head and tugged it straight. I could hear the other girls getting out of the showers, and I wanted to comb my hair in front of the mirror before the thundering herds lined up to share the one puny mirror.

"Did you hear me, Carlson?" Jinx said. She was staring right at me. "Well? Cat got your tongue, or what?"

"*Like I said* is rotten grammar." I was sorry as soon as I said it.

She hadn't pulled her sweater down yet, so the cups of her bra stuck out; she looked like she had on some sort of a weird swimsuit with arms. She stared at me as I tightened my belt. I turned around so I wouldn't have to meet her eyes.

Jinx followed me around. She'd finally pulled her sweater down and put on her jeans over her tights. She slid into her shoes. She didn't look at me, but just in my general direction. Then she reached out in a flash and pulled a hunk of my hair.

"Ow!" I yelled. I grabbed my hair and tried to get her to let go, but there wasn't enough hair for both my hands and hers. "What did you go and do that for?" I pulled my head away from her and at the same time pushed at her arms. I don't know if she got tired of pulling my hair, or if she heard someone coming, or if one of my hands hit her sore spot or what, but she let go.

" 'What did I go and do that for?' " she asked in a superprissy voice. "What do I go and do anything for? What did I go and get born for?" She lowered her voice with each sentence, so that by the end she was almost whispering. She opened her locker, took out her books, slammed the locker shut, locked it, then stormed out of the room, looking down at the floor as she passed the mirror.

"God," Peggy said, as she walked over to the locker next to mine, wearing her towel and underwear. All she'd seen was Jinx storming out in a huff after slamming the locker door.

"Probably that's what she wanted to do to Ms. Garland and didn't dare," I said. Peggy laughed. Good old Merle—always good for a laugh.

The other girls started coming in from the showers, talking and laughing and banging open their locker doors. I sat down on the wooden bench in front of my locker and started to pull on my socks. My head ached a little from where Jinx had pulled my hair, and when I tried to comb it, big hunks came out in the comb. I tossed the hair from the comb into the trash, grabbed my books and purse, and went to line up at the door until the bell rang.

I glanced into Ms. Garland's office as I passed it. There was no one inside the office; both Ms. Garland

and Jinx were gone. Just the monitor was there, standing guard.

Bronwyn Junior High wasn't so bad in seventh grade. But when I started there again in the middle of eighth grade, things had changed. My old friends had gotten into cliques with kids I didn't know, and I felt like people had forgotten me. For all they knew, I had moved away for good when I didn't show up for the first day of school. And then when I came back from Lake Lune, it was sort of like I was a new girl all over again.

Coming back was easier for my sister Diane because she was still in elementary school, so she stayed in the same class all day long with kids she'd known from before. Ron had it sort of tough, too, though. He wore a pair of jeans he'd gotten in Lake Lune to school the first day back and the snotty sixth-graders, who were in training to be supersnots in junior high the next year, started razzing him, asking where did he get the farmer's jeans? They called him hayseed and generally made him feel miserable. Ron can make a joke out of anything, but he was lower than a snake's belly after his first day back at Llewellyn Elementary.

But this Jinx Normandale was something else again. She was new to Bronwyn Junior High in eighth grade, so I didn't know anything about her except I could see that she was good in gym and that she had a smart-mouth approach to life. I'd made one good friend in Lake Lune—Mary Hauser—and I wished I could have told her all about Jinx. She would have understood.

Lake Lune was in the past, though. I couldn't afford to go calling Mary Hauser long distance. Besides, she wouldn't know what I was talking about; she'd never met Jinx Normandale—had probably never met anyone like her. And if I wrote to Mary, she might write back and tell me what Ricky and Darlene were up to these days, and I didn't think I could stand to hear about the happy couple just then. No, Lake Lune was definitely in the past.

And my sore head was definitely in the present. Goddamn that Jinx Normandale, anyway. When the bell rang, I walked as fast as I could past the monitor and out into the hall.

2

"A girl at school did this?" Grandma asked as she watched me comb out my hair. Hunks of loose hair drifted in the air as I combed.

I was sitting on a pink velvet cushion on the bench in front of her dressing table.

"You're getting hair all over the cushion, Merle."

"So?"

"So, I spent hours recovering that bench after your grandfather refinished it."

"Sorry," I said. I stood up to go into my own room.

"Oh, sit down," Grandma said. "Just try to catch the hair with your other hand when you comb, that's all."

I sat down again.

"How's school going?" Grandma asked.

It was Saturday morning and Ron and Diane were

watching cartoons. I could hear the cartoon version of Mr. T. booming at somebody.

"School's fine."

"It's so fine that girls pull your hair?"

"Just Jinx Normandale. I ignore her."

"She must be a little hard to ignore." Grandma looked at the handful of hair I was tossing into the pink wastebasket. It drifted away from the basket, and I had to bend down to get it.

The phone in the hallway rang. Grandma went to answer it.

"Hello?" she said. "Well, hello, Jack. What's up? . . . You did?" *Giggle, giggle.*

Jack must be the guy at work she'd been talking about, but Grandma giggling? *Far out.*

"You're a lumberjack now, too? . . . I know it's a bad pun, but I couldn't resist. . . . Sure, I'll bet the kids would love it. . . . Why don't you come for lunch first? . . . I've got a pot of soup on and I'm sure we can rustle up something to go with it. . . . See you then."

I started combing my hair again. I didn't want Grandma to think I was eavesdropping. Especially since I was. I tried to look very busy.

It didn't matter, though; Grandma didn't come back in. She walked down the hall to the kitchen so fast you'd think there was a fire in there. She was practically running. I was dying of curiosity, so I followed her.

"You can't comb your hair in the kitchen," she said when she saw me. "It isn't sanitary."

I stuck the comb in my jeans pocket. "So who's coming for lunch?"

She grinned. "Johann Swanson."

"I thought you called him Jack."

"Everybody does—it's his nickname."

"Oh."

She put the big Revereware Dutch oven onto the counter and then put the aluminum colander with the stars punched in it into the pot. Then she put the lid of the smaller Dutch oven into the sink and picked up the potful of soup stock. She slowly poured the whole kettle full of stock and bones into the colander. The bones and the bay leaf stayed put in the colander, and the stock drained through into the pot. Ham stock from last Sunday's ham. *Yum, yum.*

"I wonder if we've got time for split pea." She took a plastic bag of dried peas out of the cupboard and looked at it. Then she snipped one corner open with the red kitchen shears and poured the hard little peas into the stock. She put the pot back onto the stove and turned the heat on again. "Let me think here—onions, carrots, celery. . . ." She took out the vegetables and a knife and began chopping and peeling.

"How long have you known Jack?"

"He's been with the company for years, but I'd never really met him. Then we had a big cookout right after Labor Day. . . ."

"I thought you didn't like company parties. That's what you always used to say."

"Well, living alone gives you a little different view

of things. It was awful quiet around here without you kids, you know."

"What's he like?"

"You can see for yourself in about an hour. He's coming for lunch."

"How come?"

"He's going to take us out to a Christmas tree farm to cut down our tree."

"Isn't it sort of early? Christmas isn't for weeks yet."

"It's not very many Saturdays away, though. And fresh-cut trees stay good longer than the ones you buy at tree lots. So they say, anyway—I've never had one."

The sounds of "Twilight Zone" reruns came from the living room. Pretty soon Diane would come in, her eyes big as Frisbees, and say she didn't want to watch with Ron anymore because he was scaring her. Every week they did the same thing—watch cartoons and TV all Saturday morning, then fight all afternoon. You'd think they could find a better way to spend their Saturdays, but week after week it was the same thing.

We'd only been back from Lake Lune for about four Saturdays, though, and we hadn't had a TV there for —how many months? Almost five? I was afraid to get hooked on TV again. If I didn't get to liking it, no one could take it away from me. Or if they did, I wouldn't care.

". . . got three grown children," Grandma was saying. "I'm not sure if he's divorced or widowed, but his kids all live out of state."

By the time Jack came, we had the dining room table all set with a bright green tablecloth and Grandma's dishes with the yellow roses in the middle. The soup was simmering away, smelling delicious, and Grandma had made a batch of cheese muffins. We had a nice, warm, friendly lunch and then headed out to the Christmas-tree farm in Jack's station wagon.

Jack was tall and partly bald, with big blue eyes and black hair. He was about Grandma's age, but it was hard to tell.

At the Christmas-tree farm, Jack insisted that we had to get the perfect Christmas trees. We got a little "tabletop" tree for Jack first. That didn't take long. All the little trees were beautifully shaped—symmetrical and straight. But the bigger ones were lopsided and scrawny in spots. There weren't any big trees that were just bigger versions of the little trees; they all looked the worse for wear.

We traipsed on and on, looking for the perfect tree. The tree farm had rows and rows of Christmas trees, but on the edges of the big fields where they grew in rows was a real woods with hardwood trees and thick underbrush.

It was cold, but the sun shone brightly. It was already three o'clock, though, and the sun was due to plop down below the horizon in an hour or so. The sun in the winter is like a troll that peeks over the horizon for a few hours and then, quick as a wink, bobs back down again.

Jack was telling us about trolls. His parents were

from Norway and he knew lots of scary stories about trolls. Some he'd finish off in a whisper to Grandma, and they'd both chuckle together.

Finally we found the perfect tree, or at least we called it the perfect tree. It was tall, very full, and the trunk was straight. The top was tall enough for the plastic Christmas star Grandma bought the year after Mother broke all the glass ornaments on the tree. Grandma never mentioned the broken ornaments or the butcher knife Mother pulled on the paperboy, either. But, about once a Christmas, Grandma would look at the tree and cluck her tongue and say under her breath, "Just imagine—plastic ornaments."

Grandma used to have such beautiful old glass ornaments from Germany—glass balls with fat ridges to make them look like acorns; tiny, painted glass birds with brushlike tails that came out if you pulled hard enough. We always pulled the tails out and we could never get them back in. Grandma would get so mad —and then one year all the birds were broken. Striped glass balls. Swirled glass balls. Dangling pointed teardrops. The only decoration Grandma still had that I remembered from when I was a little kid was the old cloth Santa that she said she'd had on every Christmas tree since she was married. She'd carefully place him on a tree bough near the middle of the trunk of the Christmas tree each year, and she'd always pack him away first thing, before any of the other ornaments. Since he was made of cloth, he didn't break when Mother tipped over the tree—the only thing that didn't break. Even the little ceramic deer that I made in fifth grade broke when the tree crashed to the floor, because Mother thought it was sending messages. God only knows who was sending the messages or who was supposedly receiving them. Diane was across the room from me when it happened, and I'll never forget the look in her eyes when Mother shoved the tree to the floor. Diane was only five years old—just a kindergartner—and it was worse than if someone had told her there wasn't any Santa Claus. At least I was nine then; I didn't believe in Santa Claus anymore or anything. When something like that happens, you might as well make up your mind then and there that the old mom in the apron is not at home in your house.

"I think we'll probably trim the tree tomorrow afternoon, Jack," Grandma said when we got back to the house. "Would you like to stop by for some eggnog?"

"Absolutely!" Jack said. "I'll bring some brandy and we'll spike it."

The trunk of the tree was so fat that it barely fit into the Christmas-tree stand. But Jack and Ron carried it downstairs, where it stood, tall and upright and full and beautiful, right in front of the washer and dryer. It looked like it was still alive, with snow all over its boughs.

"A real beauty," Jack said. "You've got a good eye, Lily."

Grandma grinned. "I had a good guide. I wouldn't have known where to begin looking for a Christmas tree farm."

"Well, it's about time you learned," Jack said. "Those pathetic yellow things you can buy in the lots are cut in September, and they look it, too."

"Well, live and learn," Grandma said.

Jack put an arm around her shoulders. "Stick with me, kid, and I'll teach you all sorts of new tricks."

They grinned at each other, and then Jack left.

Jack came the next day and brought a bottle of blackberry brandy. Each of us got a little of the brandy, but it tasted an awful lot like sweet cough medicine.

"It's an acquired taste," Jack said, when he noticed us choking a little.

"They're too young to acquire it," Grandma said.

Jack and Ron carried the Christmas tree back up from the basement and put it in front of the picture window. Grandma had moved the rocking chair to make room for the tree. She opened the big cardboard Christmas box and began unwrapping plastic ornaments.

When we got to the bottom of the box, Jack said, "So all your ornaments are plastic, huh? I guess that's real practical when you have kids around."

"It's not because of *us*," Diane said hotly.

"Well, excu-u-u-use me," Jack said, grinning. "I didn't mean to offend you. Do you have a dog or something?"

"No. Moth—"

"Any more eggnog, anyone?" Grandma said loudly.

18

Diane looked at her. "Sure," she said.

Jack didn't stay for Sunday-night supper. He and Grandma walked together to the front door and when he left he squeezed her arm. "See you tomorrow," he said.

When she came back in, Grandma looked happy for a minute, but then she started in.

"Did you have to embarrass me?" she said to Diane. "Couldn't you leave your mother out of it just once?"

"But I stopped before I said . . ."

"Just once? Does she have to enter into everything?

"She's not even here," Diane said. "Besides, we *didn't* break the ornaments."

"She may not be here, but she's up to her old tricks again, disrupting everything."

"Just because I said something I shouldn't have? . . ."

"That's not all," Grandma said, sitting down in the recliner and leaning back so that the front raised up under her feet.

"What else did I do?" Diane asked.

"Nothing," Grandma said. "It's your mother. I got a letter yesterday that says we all have to go up north next week."

"And miss school?" Diane said.

"It won't break your heart, I'm sure," Grandma said.

"There's nothing up north," Ron said. "Just a bunch of trees and cows—"

"And your mother," Grandma said.

"Oh, *her*," Ron said. "Our friendly neighborhood lunatic."

"Don't you talk about my mother like that," Diane said.

"Who's the letter from?" I asked.

"From a court," Grandma said. "Your mother apparently has demanded to have a jury trial to determine whether she should stay in the hospital or be released. And the judge agrees with her."

"That she should get out?"

"Well, no. I don't think anyone thinks that—"

"Except Mother," Ron said.

"You're right," Grandma said. "She apparently still doesn't think she's sick. But she is demanding to see her children, and the judge says she has that right."

"What are we supposed to tell the school?" I asked.

"I'll write you a note," Grandma said. "But I'm not going to go into details. What happens at home stays at home."

"But it's happening in Lake Lune," Diane pointed out.

"No, the courthouse is in Muskeegoom," Grandma said.

"That's still not at home."

"I think it's time someone around here did the dishes," Grandma said. "And then it's time for baths and bed."

"Can't we turn the tree lights on? Just for a minute?" Diane asked.

"*No*," Grandma said sharply. "It's late." But then she looked over at Diane. "Oh, I guess so. You plug them in, Ron."

We all sat in the dark living room for a minute and looked at the lights on the tree. There were three tall bubble lights—yellow for Diane, blue for Ron, red for me. The three primary colors that all the other colors come from. Red and yellow and blue. Who would ever think so many colors could come from so few?

It took a minute for them to start bubbling. The light reflected through the liquid in each column and then slowly, one by one, tiny bubbles started at the bottoms and floated up. Everything seemed to go in and out of focus—the crystals studding the snowball lights, the twinklers winking on and off, the tinsel garlands reflecting but distorting everything.

Back up to Wisconsin. Oh God. Would we have to see her? What would she be like? What would she say?

I stared at the little cloth Santa who flopped in the tree like a clown or a drunk. But he was old and he'd seen all of Grandma's Christmases since she got married.

It must be scary to get married. You never know what's going to happen or how your kids will turn out or whether you'll be rich or poor.

All those gorgeous glass ornaments and now all Grandma had left was a crummy cotton Santa. His suit had faded to pink and his face was blurred. Who knew what he used to look like or why Grandma picked him for her very first tree?

3

"We're going to crash!" Grandma yelled. She jerked the steering wheel to the right and the car skidded over onto the shoulder. Her right foot in its furry snow boot was pressed hard against the brake. I stared at her boot; I couldn't look at the highway.

Diane screamed, "I'm too young to die!"

Icy gravel crunched under the wheels of the car until finally we stopped. I looked up in time to see the trailer roar off, its rows of tires spitting ice at us.

"There ought to be a law," Ron said.

"There probably is," I said. There we were, sitting on a highway somewhere in Wisconsin in an ice storm, discussing laws made by people we didn't know, in a state where we didn't live.

Grandma had leaned her forehead on the steering wheel and slumped her shoulders down over it.

"Christ," we could hear her say. "All I need is an accident. That's all I need."

"It's okay," Diane said. "Grandma, look, we're safe."

"Relatively speaking," Ron said.

"*Except* for our relatives," I said, and we giggled.

Grandma sat halfway up again. "Maybe one of you would like to drive," she said.

"Sure," Ron said. "I'll drive; I'd be great at it."

"You're only eleven," I said. "At least I'm thirteen —maybe I should drive."

"I'm getting out of here if you drive, Merle," Diane said. "You can't even steer the carts in the grocery store straight."

"I don't believe my ears," Grandma said. "Here we are, stuck on some godforsaken highway in the middle of weather like this, late for an important appointment, and you're joking around."

"Yeah, well, we have to do something to keep our minds off our worries," Ron said. "How would you like to go to *your* mother's trial?"

"My mother's dead," Grandma said. "And it's no picnic to go to your *daughter's* trial, either . . . I mean . . . I thought I told you kids it's *not* a trial," she said, starting to shout again. "It's a hearing to determine . . . oh, the hell with it."

She straightened her shoulders and started the car. After she'd looked twice back over her left shoulder to be sure no cars were coming, she put on her turn signal and drove slowly back onto the highway.

23

You've got to hand it to Grandma—she's a good driver.

"Sit up straight, Merle," she said. "You'll get curvature of the spine if you slouch around like that."

I shifted in the front seat. Usually Ron and Diane fight too much to be alone in the backseat together, but this morning we were all too tired to think much about the seating arrangements when we piled into the car at 6:00 A.M. It was still pitch dark when we left Chicago, and the car windows were white with frost. The car was warmed up now from the car heater, and the frost had melted. And, instead of being sleepy, we were all on edge from the excitement that comes from too little sleep and too much worry.

"This highway is just murderous," Grandma said. "I can't believe I'm doing this . . . and for her, of all people."

"You leave my mother alone," Diane said.

"Ha!" Grandma said. "Tell her to leave *me* alone. I'm not the one who's making her drive hundreds of miles for some stupid hearing that shouldn't even be happening in the first place."

"It's not her fault she's stuck up there," Diane said. She looked as though she were going to cry.

"It most certainly *is* her fault," Grandma said. "Who made her take off for a tent in Lake Lune and camp out for the summer with three poor little innocent children?"

The three of us groaned.

"No running water," Grandma said. "Not even a flush toilet. . . ."

"We were there, Grandma," I pointed out. "It wasn't all bad, you know."

"No decent clothes," Grandma went on. "And then that house she moved you into last fall was so crummy no farmer would put horses in it."

"Can we listen to the radio for a while, Grandma?" Ron asked. "Maybe we can still pick up WLS from Chicago."

Grandma looked at him in the rearview mirror. "Nice manners, Ronald," she said. "In my day, we were taught to be seen and not heard."

"A thousand pardons," Ron said. He clapped one hand over his mouth and made mumbling noises. Diane giggled and reached over to try to pry his fingers off his mouth. Naturally, he pushed her away and then started tickling her, and they got pretty loud.

"If you two don't stop that this instant, I'm pulling off the road and you can walk to Muskeegoom," Grandma said.

"Right," Ron said. "We'll hitch a ride—boom, boom, we're on our way to Muskeegoom."

"But I didn't even bring a scarf," whined Diane. "I thought we'd be in the car all day."

"Ah, we'd get a ride right away with a sign that said: LOONY BIN OR BUST," Ron said.

"I'll bet," I said. "People don't like to think about that kind of stuff, you know, Ron."

"I wonder what she'll look like," Diane said.

"Blond hair," Ron said. "Blue eyes. Red skin."

"Will you cut it out, Ron?" I said. "Just cut it out."

"Sensitive, sensitive," Ron said, leaning over the seat and looking at me. "You've got a few junior-grade zits there, too, I see. Hitting close to home, huh?"

Usually my face only broke out when I got my period, but I hadn't had it for months. I wasn't about to tell Ron that. Let alone Grandma. She'd probably have had a heart attack if I'd said it out loud in the car. Of course, Grandma knew about periods—she must have menstruated herself, or how could she have had babies—but it wasn't the kind of word she'd ever say out loud.

"I don't want to hear anything more out of any of you the rest of the trip, *period*," Grandma said.

I started to cough and I couldn't stop.

"I don't see what's so funny, Merle," Grandma said.

"I'm not laughing," I said. "I'm choking."

"It sounds like laughing to me," Grandma said.

"Will we get to go in today?" Diane asked.

"It will be no place for children," Grandma said. "I'll find someplace for you three kids to sit and read."

"Well, then I don't see why *we* had to come," Ron said. "It's not exactly Paris in the springtime." He pointed out toward the gray sky and the scraggly evergreens we were passing.

"We've been over this and over this," Grandma said. "Your mother insisted that I bring you. Elaine hasn't got the sense she was born with, but if they tell me I have to bring you because it's Elaine's right, I'm damned if I'll defy the court."

"We could have written her a letter."

"I'm not going to let your mother accuse me of kidnapping you kids or something. I've heard enough of that kind of crap to last me a lifetime."

"And what about us?" Diane said. "We have feelings, too, you know."

"Oh, boo-hoo," Ron said. "Bring in the violins."

"Well, she never got to see us to say good-bye, you know," I said.

"She probably didn't even notice," Ron said.

"Watch for signs," Grandma said.

"What?" Ron said. "Don't tell me you're going off the deep end, too."

"*That's it,*" Grandma said. "I've had enough! I'll take you to the courthouse and drop you off, and I'll let the court decide what to do with the three of you, too."

There was a truly loud silence in the car. The wind whistled as it blew snow snakes across the icy highway. All four of us stared at the snow and the ugly billboards sticking up high above the trees way off the sides of the highway.

I began to wish I'd packed a suitcase and sneaked it into the trunk of the car. I thought back to all those months in Lake Lune with nothing decent to wear. I'd just gotten used to having my own clothes around again when Grandma had to start making threats. She couldn't mean it, but it made me nervous to hear her talk like that, anyway.

I looked down at my blue jeans. I'd worn my warmest clothes—jeans, with tights underneath. Boots. A turtleneck ski sweater that was too tight to wear over a blouse anymore. A black cardigan sweater over that. My parka with the fake fur-lined hood. Gloves and a wool hat. To say nothing of the blue bandanna I'd wound around my head so my hair wouldn't show. Damn Jinx Normandale, anyway. Double damn her to hell and back.

"You can borrow my wool hat," I said to Diane. Her jacket didn't have a hood.

"What?" she said. "Why would I want to do that?"

"So your ears won't get cold," I said. "In case we have to walk far."

"Thanks, Merle," she said, and took down the blanket from the back window of the car. She shook it out and tucked it around her legs.

"You cold, honey?" Grandma said. "I could turn up the heater."

"Uh, that's okay," Diane said.

Ron gave me a look. Diane was directly behind me, so I couldn't meet her eyes, but Ron's were filled with a shine that might have been a twinkle; he could make a joke out of anything. But the shine looked too thick to be a twinkle; it looked like it might drip down his cheeks.

I turned back around and stared out my side of the

window. I didn't want to look at Grandma. There wasn't much to see except ice, trees, billboards, and snow snaking along the highway. We passed a sign that said: FLY FREE AIR AND SMILE YOUR WAY SOUTH. Driving north, the only entertainment was watching the snow snakes and trying to figure out strange people and strange events; no wonder people want to fly south. During Wisconsin in the winter, they should ban those signs about Florida.

"Signs!" I said. It sounded very loud, since everything had been so quiet.

"Not you, too," Ron said.

"That's what you meant, isn't it, Grandma? Road signs."

"Well, of course," she said. "I'm looking for the sign that says Muskeegoom."

"I think we just found it," Ron said. And sure enough, there was a big green road sign up ahead that said: EXIT MUSKEEGOOM, ¾ MILE.

Grandma took the exit ramp and drove slowly until we got to a sign that said: MUSKEEGOOM, POP. 5,124. She speeded up a little then. "Imagine driving around looking for a courthouse," she said, very softly. "Just imagine."

I kept thinking about the last time I'd seen Mother, in her bare feet and tangled hair. It had been snowing then, too. It was only a month ago, but it seemed like a year. We'd been back in Chicago and going to school as though nothing had happened.

That was the hardest thing for me to get used to. It

was like living in Lake Lune all over again, only more comfortable.

When Mother was around, we couldn't pretend she didn't exist. But with Mother in the hospital in Wisconsin, and us back in Bronwyn right outside of Chicago, it was sort of like she didn't exist. Kids at school don't sit around asking you about your parents— you're supposed to have better things to talk about by the time you hit the big-time teenage years. Even adults say nice nothings like, "Glad to see you're back —how's school going?"

Not that I wanted to go into the whole story of Mother's mental problems, but it sure seemed weird to have five months of my life just drop out of sight like that. The other times Mother had had breakdowns we'd go through the whole three-ring circus with her, then she'd get shipped off to the hospital and we'd go back to our real lives.

It's hard when you have to consider part of your life not real, though. I mean, Mother was real enough. She talked like a real person. She wasn't a mechanical toy, even though she had to go get fixed up every once in a while. Sometimes it seemed like everybody would rather pretend that she didn't even exist. Maybe for other people, if they pretended that Elaine Carlson didn't exist—poof, she was gone. But I could pretend until the cows come home, yet she'd one day come home again. She wasn't a bad dream to me; she was my mother. She had custody of me. She was in charge of all three of us.

"Here we are," Grandma said, stopping the car in a slanted parking place and pulling the emergency brake so hard it squeaked. "Let's get going. We're ten minutes late as it is."

We got out of the car, locked the doors, and zipped up our coats as we walked across the parking lot. Ridges of frozen slush cut into the soles of our boots. You could see that the slush had been squishing around not too long ago. It was different shades of gray and yellow, dirt and ice and water and dog pee all mixed together, and then frozen into little peaks where the cold had caught it.

We had to walk up three flights of concrete steps just to get to the courthouse, which was on a sort of a knoll or little hill. From the parking lot, it looked like something out of *Frankenstein*—a huge, looming red-brick building with eaves and curlicues and enormous windows like square, blank eyes. The steps had been chopped out of the side of the hill, and they went back and forth at weird angles up the hill. The concrete was lined with varicose cracks, and the black iron pipes that were handrails were rusted and peeling. Your basic spiffy public institution this was not. It looked like it had been left out in the rain too long, or like it should never have been built.

"Here we go," Grandma said, as she opened the big black-painted wooden door and waited for us to scoot in ahead of her. "Make me proud of you, sweethearts," she said. "We're all a little tense this morning, but we'll make it fine."

31

I think she was trying to say she was sorry, but with so many things for all of us to feel sorry about, it's hard to know just what she had in mind.

The door was heavier than it looked and its springs must have been broken. It slammed shut behind us as we stood in the dim hallway, letting our eyes get accustomed to the pale yellow light inside.

"Oh, no!" Diane said.

"What's wrong?" Grandma asked.

"She's not here."

We all four looked down the long, wide hallway. It was paneled in dark wood. The only lights were in the ceiling, high above us. The floor was black-speckled linoleum. There was a lot of linoleum showing; the only furniture in the hall, which was as wide as the length of most living rooms, was a few high wooden benches with their backs to the walls, a few chrome-plated ashtrays on stands with handles on top, and two big radiators. Plus a porcelain drinking fountain decorated with rust marks.

"Jesus, is this the pits or what?" Ron said.

"There's nobody here at all," Diane said. "Where's Mommy?"

"I wish I knew," Grandma said. "I'm always the last to find out anything. Who am *I*, anyway? Just the grandmother."

She stood there for a while looking around the hall, and then she walked quickly over to a door that had just opened. Actually, only the top half of the door was open. It was a Dutch door, and the woman on the other side must have been sitting down because you could see her face, but not the rest of her.

We three kids walked over to one of the radiators and stood there to warm up. On the wall above us was a painting of a man in a suit and tie who looked as though he sold something sleazy for a living.

Grandma walked back toward us, squaring her shoulders and raising her head high. "We're all set," she said. "You three can wait out here in the hall and I'll go in now. See that bench over there?" She pointed to one of the high wooden benches that lined the hallway. "Just sit tight. I'll be back as soon as I can." She gave us each a little pat on the cheek and looked us each in the face, as though she were trying to memorize what we looked like, and then she took off down the hall, her boots squeaking softly against the linoleum.

People walked down the hall from time to time, but no one stopped to talk to us or even look at us. The light was rotten for reading, so we sat and stared as people passed by. After a while, a big crowd walked past us. In the middle of the whole crowd I thought I saw Mother, but I couldn't quite tell. They all went through another door before we had a chance to get up and see.

"Diane, I think that was Mother," I whispered, when the hall was empty again.

"I wonder why she didn't say hi to us," Diane said. "It wouldn't've hurt her."

"She had lots of things on her mind," I said. "Or maybe she didn't see us."

"Wouldn't be the first time," Ron said.

"Maybe she forgot who we were," I said. "That used to happen sometimes, too."

"Don't remind me," Ron said. "Just about anything used to happen." He rolled his eyes, as though he were watching old movies on the backs of his eyelids.

"Still does," I said. "I never thought we'd be sitting here right now, for instance."

A man walked slowly by, looking at us as he walked. We all stopped talking. Diane got out her coloring book and held it in her lap. Ron had some comic books along. I'd brought *A Tree Grows in Brooklyn*, but I wished I had something else to read. Francie Nolan was too close to home just then.

After the man opened a door and walked out, we put our books down again.

We sat and listened to the big clock on the wall go *tick, tick, tick*, as though every second was important. Maybe in a courthouse every second is important. In the rest of the world, though, days—even years—can go by without anybody even knowing the difference. *Tick, tick, tick.*

The big wooden door opened suddenly, and Grandma came out. We all looked at her and Diane jumped up.

"Did you see her?" she asked. "Did you see my mommy?"

"Yes," Grandma said. "She's in the courtroom right now. She wants to talk to Merle."

"Merle!" Ron and Diane said together, loudly.

"Me?" I said. I felt like someone had woken me up in the middle of a dream and said, Here, quick eat these Cheerios. It didn't make any sense to me, and all I could say was, "Why me?"

"I ask myself that all the time," Grandma said. "Why me? And I never come up with any answers."

"But I don't want . . ." I started to say.

"What about us?" asked Diane. "Why can't we see Mother?"

"Oh, don't start all this fussing," Grandma said. "You all three will get to see your mother after the hearing is over. This is just another one of your mother's crazy ideas," she said, her voice rising. "Come on, Merle. You don't have to talk to her long."

I stood up and straightened my bandanna and pulled my sweater down so it covered the tops of my jeans. I followed Grandma through the big dark door into the courtroom. I felt I had to walk tall and brave, like I was on TV or something. Only instead of the glamorous lady lawyer on "Hill Street Blues," I was some weirdo from "That's Incredible!"

The walls of the courtroom were creamy green, and

the American flag hung next to what must have been the flag of Wisconsin. There were people milling around the room and the judge wasn't there—at least so far as I could tell. He could have been one of the men in business suits, I suppose, but I always thought judges wore long, black robes, and there was no one in the room wearing a long, black robe.

No one even looked up when I walked into the courtroom with Grandma. Everyone was busy whispering to everyone else, and I saw Mother sitting at a table talking to a man in a polyester plaid suit. He looked pretty tacky to me, but then I guess you can't really tell much about people from their clothes. I wouldn't want to be judged by some of the outfits I wore in Lake Lune—when we had two crummy outfits each—that's for sure.

Grandma left me by myself in the side aisle of the courtroom, and she went over and sat down on one of the benches. I wished she'd leave the room, if she wasn't going to stand next to me. It made me nervous to have her just far enough away that I couldn't tell if she could hear or not.

I stood there until Mother noticed me. She poked the man's arm and he looked around at me, too. Neither of them smiled or said anything, so I kept standing there. Finally, they both got up and walked over to me.

"Hello, Merle," Mother said, very softly. She bent over and very stiffly kissed my cheek. Then she stiffly stood upright again.

"Hello, Mother." I stood on tiptoes to kiss her cheek. She seemed shorter than the last time I'd seen her, only a month before. Her skin looked pale, but red underneath, like she had a reverse tan. "How are you?"

"What kind of a question is that when you see me in a place like this? How do you think I am?"

I just said, "Um, well, um, well," and tried to wait her out. If you don't try to get the better of Mother in conversations, sometimes she'll get nervous herself and start talking. I thought it was only fair; after all, I hadn't asked to see *her*.

"It's too public here," Mother said. "Can't we go somewhere private to talk?" She looked at me as she said this, but it was obvious that she was talking to the man next to her.

He gave her a peculiar look—an are-you-crazy-lady? look—and said, no, we really couldn't leave the courtroom.

"Well, maybe we could go stand behind those high benches over there," she said.

"You mean the jury box?" he said, pronouncing slowly as though she were a child.

So we walked over behind the jury box and had a sort of a huddle. I was facing out toward the rows of benches in the main part of the courtroom, though, and I could see Grandma clear as anything. She wasn't exactly looking at me, but I knew she knew I was back there. I had a feeling she looked at me when I wasn't looking her way.

"Merle," Mother said. "This is Mr. Sarow, my lawyer."

Of course I had to say, "How do you do," and smile at him. He smiled back, but not very convincingly.

"Well," I said, "so when did you inherit money?"

Mother glared at me. "Just what do you mean by that?"

"I thought lawyers were expensive."

"I'm a public defender," the lawyer said, as though that explained anything.

"I would like you to tell Mr. Sarow exactly what happened the day we left Chicago for Lake Lune," Mother said.

"Why?" I said.

"Don't sass me, young lady. Do as I say." Mother's eyes stared into mine, as though she could control even whether I would blink or not.

I finally did blink. In fact, I fluttered my eyelids for a while so I didn't have to look at her. But when I opened my eyes wide again, there she was, her eyes steady and so blue that if they were a lake you'd drown in them. "But I don't understand what's . . ." I said.

"Your mother—" Mr. Sarow said, but Mother interrupted him.

"Your grandmother is trying to get them to lock me up and throw away the key."

"But you're already . . ." I said.

She jerked her body sideways like a broken ballerina on a jewelry box. "I've been in that hellhole for a month now!" she half-whispered, half-shouted.

"There is nothing the matter with me! I'm as sane as you are!" She grabbed my arm and squeezed tight. "Every bit as sane as you are, Merle Glenda Carlson. How would you like it if I had you locked up?"

I looked down at my boots. There was a white line where the salt from the snow had crept up the black suede. "I wouldn't."

"Louder!" she hissed.

I looked at her. "There's nothing wrong with me, Mother."

"There's nothing wrong with me, either. Ask Mr. Sarow. We just need your help in convincing the judge."

"But I'm not a doctor," I said. Neither was Mr. Sarow, but I didn't see any point in mentioning that.

"I don't need a doctor!" Mother said. "That's the last thing I need. I need my freedom. I need to be with my babies."

If Ron had been there, he'd have said she was really pouring it on. If Diane had been there, she'd probably have fallen for the babies crap. But I couldn't think of a thing to say.

"The judge will understand that I acted in the best interests of my children when you tell him what happened in Chicago on the sixth of July."

"He will?" I said.

"I went to Lake Lune for my own protection and that of my children." Mother had calmed down a little and was using her princess voice.

Mr. Sarow cleared his throat. He'd been looking at

the clock during this whole bizarre scene and now he said, "There's not much time left."

Mother ignored him, but her voice changed from a princess's to a beggar's. "You are my oldest child, Merle. I'm counting on you. I don't have anyone else." This time she looked at Mr. Sarow while she talked to me.

"Your grandmother went completely berserk and chased us out of the house. I was frightened to return and left for Lake Lune, because I didn't dare risk taking my children back there," Mother said.

Mr. Sarow was looking down at his shoes, which were black, the color of the linoleum. They had white salt lines and sprinkles of road salt all over them, worse than mine. He licked his forefinger and reached down to wipe off some of the salt.

"That's disgusting," I said.

He jerked back upright. "You mean it isn't true? Your grandmother didn't do that?"

"I meant wiping off your shoe with spit like that."

"Mind your manners," Mother said. "Pretty is as pretty does, even if you do look like a fieldhand with that rag around your head."

"I'm a person, not a doll, Mother!"

"You're my baby doll, and you always will be."

"No! I won't!"

"Merle Glenda Carlson, you tell Mr. Sarow what you saw."

"No," I said.

"Merle," she said, squeezing my arm again, "have

you no loyalty? Don't you love your own mother?"

"Stop it! I can't stand it."

"Don't you start that crybaby stuff. That's not going to get me out of the hospital. Did your grandmother, or did she not, kick me when I was down on the floor picking up the pieces of my purse, which she had broken?"

What would happen if I told the truth? Would they let her go? Would Grandma disown me?

"Well?" said Mr. Sarow, impatiently.

"It's hard to remember," I said.

It wasn't though. I could see, plain as day, Grandma kicking Mother. I could remember Grandma saying, "Then pay me what you owe me!" *Kick. Kick. Kick.* I could remember Mother screeching like a bird.

"Well?" Mother said. I didn't look at her. "You got a cigarette?" she asked Mr. Sarow.

I guess she figured he might answer her, if I wouldn't.

He took out a crumpled package of cigarettes and a blue lighter and handed them to Mother. She didn't take them, though. Finally, he pulled out a cigarette and handed it to her, then lit the cigarette with the lighter. She inhaled, as though the smoke was the best thing she'd ever had in her life. Then she lifted her head and looked around the courtroom, her lungs filled with smoke. Finally, she exhaled and then looked at me.

"It was a long time ago now, you know," I said. "I sort of . . ."

"*Merle,*" Mother said. She stared at me with her hypnotizing look, trying to force me to tell the truth. "It wasn't that long ago, Merle. We were in our own cozy little house in Lake Lune just a month ago."

Little, you could call our house in Lake Lune. But cozy? With no furniture, no curtains, no hot water, no nothing?

"And I kept it clean, too," Mother said to Mr. Sarow.

I thought of her, the last night we were there, "washing the floor" with an old T-shirt and cold water. "Filthy, evil bastards aren't going to poison me with drugs ever again. . . . They're not getting you. I won't let them have you. I'd rather see you in your— my poor babies."

That was only a month ago—how could she be well already? Would the judge take her word for it if I backed her up?

I looked her right smack in the eye. "No, Mother, it wasn't very long ago."

"We don't have all day," Mr. Sarow said. "The docket is . . ."

"Will you leave this poor child alone?" Mother said. "Can't you see how upset she is? Give her a minute to collect herself; then she'll tell us the truth. She's a good girl. You'll see."

"What's the docket?" I asked the lawyer.

He didn't answer me. He took another cigarette out of his shirt pocket and lit it. His blue plastic lighter said: HEART OF THE NORTHLAND. It had a tiny red heart on the side. He turned around to look when a door opened at the front of the courtroom and a bunch of people walked in. "Judge's back," he said. "You got anything at all to say about what happened that day you left Chicago?"

All the years living with Mother had taught me something about how to make weird situations look normal. In a way it was Mother's fault I answered the way I did. It was because of her that I knew so well how to make bizarre stories sound ordinary.

"They had an argument that morning," I said. I didn't look at Mother or the lawyer. I looked at a corner of the wooden jury box. I kept expecting Mother to interrupt me, and I spoke very slowly to give her the chance to do it.

"I guess Mother hadn't paid the rent yet and it was the fourth of July already and Grandma sort of lost her temper 'cause I guess she needed the money."

Mother didn't say a word, not even to correct my mistake about the date. She didn't even look at me. She must have figured out what I was going to do.

Mr. Sarow looked at me as though I were a poster for a movie he didn't want to see, and he didn't say anything, either. I had to finish up without the help of interruptions from anybody. ". . . So they argued about money for a while until we left," I said.

"And then where did you go?" he asked.

"Lake Lune, in Wisconsin," I said. "I thought you knew that."

"But you went without taking any extra clothes?"

"We bought a suitcase," I said. "Just one suitcase for the four of us, but of course it was big. And then we bought clothes once we got there."

"Uh, well, thanks, Merle," Mr. Sarow said. He almost seemed relieved. I suppose it was easier for him if he thought Mother had been lying or crazy than if he'd had to fight hard for her because he thought she wasn't.

"Yeah," I said. "Good-bye, Mr. Sorrow."

"It's Sarow, with an *a* and just one *r*," he said. "Well, good-bye." He turned and started back toward the front of the courtroom.

I stood there watching him go. Mother started to follow him, but then she turned around and stared at me until I looked up at her.

"You know what you've done, Merle," she said. "You'll have to live with it."

Grandma was busy talking to a woman in high heels and a business suit. I couldn't think of anything else to do but walk back out to the hallway and sit with Ron and Diane again. I pushed on the door with my side for a minute, but it wouldn't budge. Then I saw it had a brass handle and as soon as I turned that, it opened. I was back out in the hall, with the door slamming shut behind me.

5

Diane and Ron were sitting on the bench, reading and chatting just as though nothing had happened. Nothing had happened—to them. I was the one who had betrayed my mother. I figured from the way Mr. Sarow had looked at me and what Mother had said that she had no other defense. She had insisted on this stupid jury trial, which Grandma said was her right according to the Constitution but not for any other sane reason. I had to agree with Grandma on that one. Mother was going to lose, lose, lose, just like she always lost, lost, lost. And I had helped it happen.

"What did she want?" Diane asked as soon as I got back to the bench where they still sat, waiting.

"Oh, well," I said. "She just wanted me to meet her lawyer."

"Why?" Ron asked.

"Uh, well, I'm not really sure," I said. "You know how she is." That's all I needed to say; they figured it was just another one of her crazy ideas. It probably was, but in some whole different way that made me feel lousy and alone.

"I still think she could have asked to see all three of us," Diane said. "It's just like always—you're her pet. Perfect little Merle."

"Shut up, Diane," I said. "You don't have a clue how horrible it was in there."

"Rub it in," she said. "Who cares how anybody else feels, so long as Merle gets her way."

I took out *A Tree Grows in Brooklyn*. Even Francie's aunt's stillbirths couldn't be as awful as this. In fact, a stillbirth or two sounded like a wonderful idea just then. If Mother hadn't had us, maybe she would have been spared all this; or at least we would have been.

So we sat there. And sat there. I could hear Diane coloring in her book. She took out first one crayon, used it for a while, then carefully put it back and chose another. She's the artistic one in the family. She was working on a medieval scene, with knights and ladies-in-waiting and unicorns.

I tried to read, but I couldn't concentrate. All I could think about was the way Mother had looked at me at first, and then how she wouldn't look at me at all, and then how she said I'd have to live with what I'd said. Maybe she was right. You don't forget that sort of thing very fast.

And the way Mr. Sarow had looked at Mother had

made me feel even worse. He probably thought she was just some sort of an idiot or something. He didn't know anything about any of her good qualities, or the fact that not all the things that have happened to her in her life have been her fault. He probably thought she was just some creep off the street who neglected her children and whose daughter was a liar.

He must have known I'd been lying. How could I have just out-and-out lied like that? And yet, if it hadn't been for Mr. Sarow, I don't think I would have cared so much. Of course, if it had been just Mother and me, I never would have said what I said. Why should I care what he thought of me, anyway? After all, I'll never see him again, and I suppose I'll have to keep seeing my mother over and over again forever.

Ron and Diane and I were getting really stiff and bored from sitting there all that time. We could hear a typewriter; sometimes a telephone rang somewhere. Life was going on; people were just going about their business as though nothing were happening. It was only happening to us. And, really, it wasn't even happening to us—it was happening to Mother.

We sat there for a long time, nobody saying a word. Finally a woman who had walked by carrying papers a couple of times came over and started to talk to us. She had a paper sack. She took out a bag of candy orange slices from it and gave it to us. I expected that she'd start pumping us about Mother, but she didn't. She just mentioned how chilly it was, and asked where we were from, and said she hoped we wouldn't have to sit in the hall by ourselves much longer. Then she left us alone with the bag of orange slices.

It was a whole pound bag. Ron ripped a hole in the plastic with his teeth and then pulled a bigger opening. The orange slices were gooey orange jelly with crusted sugar all over the outsides. They were fat and crescent shaped, with scalloped ridges along the top. They looked like fat slugs that in some other life might have been ugly and slimy, but sparkled and were sweet in this one.

We ate them down, every single one. An orange slice totally fills your mouth at first. As you chew and the saliva begins to flow, it gets smaller and smaller, and slides down your throat, sweet warm goo.

When we got down to the four last orange slices in the bag, we had to decide who got the extra one.

"Maybe we should try 'Eine, Sveine, Klein, horse-'n'-goggle,' " I suggested.

"Don't you mean 'horse-'n'-*gobble*'?" Ron said.

"I don't get it," Diane said. "What's 'horse-'n'-gobble'?"

So we showed her how to make fists and count out "Eine, Sveine, Klein," and then, on "horse-'n'-goggle," to put up either one, two, or three fingers. Whoever puts up a number no one else has is the winner. It works better with lots of people, though. Finally, Ron and Diane each put up three fingers and I put up one.

"You win," Diane said. "Just like always."

I took one orange slice out of the bag and handed the

other three to Diane. "You take the extra one," I said. "I don't want it, anyway."

"I don't believe it," she said, putting her hand into the bag and taking out two pieces of candy. "Amazing."

Ron took the last piece and put it on his knee while he tried to blow up the plastic bag like a balloon. He cupped his hands around the hole. He made the opening as small as possible and then blew and blew into the bag. It puffed up into a fat rectangle. Ron's face got redder and redder, and just as I was beginning to worry that he'd pop a blood vessel or something, he took his hands away from his mouth, squeezed the opening of the bag tight with one hand, and smashed the bag into the open palm of his other hand as hard as he could.

The *pop* of the bag echoed down the hallway. People came running to look at what had happened. When they saw the three of us laughing our heads off and the exploded plastic bag on the floor, they shook their heads and went away again.

Ron's last orange slice had fallen to the floor in all the excitement, so he picked it up and rinsed it off under the water from the white porcelain drinking fountain. Then he popped it into his mouth, dripping wet.

I hadn't eaten my last orange slice, either, but it was melting in my hand. I popped it into my mouth, but instead of chewing it up, I sucked on it. My tongue went back and forth, back and forth, working the candy from a solid to a liquid that slithered down my throat.

We sat and stared at the popped bag on the floor and listened to far-off telephones ringing and typewriters typing. All of a sudden the courtroom doors burst open and a bunch of people came out. Some walked one way and some the other. Grandma finally came out and walked fast toward us.

"Let's go," she said.

"But what about Mother?" asked Diane.

Grandma looked at her. "How'd you get that stain on your sweater?" she asked. "Orange will never come out of yellow, you know."

Diane stared back. "You promised we could see Mommy today."

"I didn't promise anything."

"Mommy is here and you said we could see her."

"Merle saw her," Grandma said. She leaned down and picked up the plastic bag. "Where'd this come from?"

"Just because Merle is everybody's pet. . . . It isn't fair!" Diane said.

"Somebody came by and gave us a bag of orange slices," I said.

"You took candy from a stranger?" Grandma said.

Diane stood up and walked toward the courtroom door. "I'm going to find her," she said.

Grandma followed after her. "She's not in there."

"She couldn't have vanished into thin air," Ron said. "She must be in there."

"Well, she's not," Grandma said. "There are two doors, and I saw her go out the front one with my own eyes."

"Grandma, you promised," Diane said.

"I am not in charge of the world," Grandma said through her teeth. "I can't make everything perfect for you. Let's get going, and we'll stop for lunch along the way."

"We're not very hungry," we all said, almost in unison.

"Well, *I am*," Grandma said. "You could think about somebody else besides yourselves, you know." She still had the plastic bag in one hand, and she was buttoning her coat with the other. She started walking toward the door we'd come in.

We followed her, putting on our jackets. She tossed the popped plastic bag into the wastebasket on the way out.

In the car, no one had much to say. We finally stopped for hamburgers, milk, and coffee for Grandma. She bought a newspaper and read while she ate. Probably she didn't want us to ask her what had gone on in the courtroom. From what I'd seen, I could understand why, but Ron and Diane probably couldn't.

I sat in the front seat of the car on the way home, too. My head ached from the tight bandanna, and I kept thinking about what kind of a rotten person would lie about her mother and get her hair pulled at school. What was wrong with me? At least in Lake

Lune, kids had liked me and Mother hadn't had public defender lawyers giving me the third degree and juries deciding her—and my—fate. Maybe my period would never start again and it would be my punishment. For being such a rotten daughter, I'd never get to be a mother myself.

I put my knee up under my chin until Grandma said, "You're dripping."

"What?" I said. For some reason I thought she meant my period had started, but how could she know that? "What are you talking about?"

She gave me a look and pointed at my boot on the car seat. "The snow is melting," she said. "What else would I mean?"

My skull throbbed. *Press. Press. Press. Drip. Drip. Drip.* I put my foot back down next to the other one on the car floor and stared out at the gray light.

After a while we saw an orange-and-turquoise HoJo's and stopped for Cokes. Everybody in the restaurant looked so regular and ordinary—even us. I felt like I should have a big green *L* for liar emblazoned on my forehead, but of course there wasn't. There was just a tiny red zit that was either getting bigger or going away; I couldn't tell which.

6

Monday morning Jinx Normandale wore an eyepatch to school. I heard someone ask her what had happened to her eye, and she said, "I walked into a door, stupid." She pushed her bangs farther down over her eyes. We were all on our way into study hall, where Mr. Stricker walked around with a wooden ruler that he hit against the edges of tables and chairs. The rumor was that once he'd hit his ruler against a desk so hard it had split and blinded a kid in the front row, but it's kind of hard to take that kind of thing too seriously. Still, you wouldn't want to be on his blacklist.

"Had a little accident, did we?" he said to Jinx as she walked by him. She looked down at the floor, then shook her head so that her bangs wiggled.

"No? You hurt your eye on *purpose?*" he said, sounding astonished.

She didn't answer, just kept walking toward her seat. Stricker followed her, his ruler raised. As she turned to sit down, Jinx caught sight of the ruler. She kind of jumped and then melted down into the chair, her good eye aimed at the table, as though she could be invisible to Stricker if she didn't look at him.

"I've had some dandy shiners in my day," he said. "*I* never wore an eyepatch, either. You in some sort of a cat fight, or what?"

When she still wouldn't answer him, he finally gave up and walked down the rows, his wooden ruler rising and falling.

"Shit," Jinx said, under her breath. She turned toward me. I was on her right, next to her good eye. She looked sort of pathetic sitting there in her weird clothes and eyepatch, but I ignored her.

I heard someone whisper, "He's such a jerk—just forget it."

"Easy for you to say," she whispered back. "He's not picking on you."

Just then Stricker turned again and faced the back of the room. I started reading the *Cooking for Living* textbook: "Niacin is . . . ." I peeked over at Jinx. She had a remedial math book open—but she was holding it upside down. When she noticed me looking at her, she stared down at the book. After a few seconds, she put the book down flat open and then slowly rotated it until it was right side up.

I forgot all about Jinx until the bell rang. Then I got up, picked up my books, and started out the door. Jinx

cut me off and went through the door first, just as
Stricker said, "Hey, you!" I ignored him, but he said
it again.

I turned around. "Me?"

He looked me straight in the face. "No, not you," he
said in disgust. "Her." He pointed toward Jinx, who
was hotfooting it down the hall.

"Oh," I said. "Well, I've got to get to my next class."

I walked down the hall the other direction, thinking
about Jinx's eye. Had she been fighting with another
girl? It didn't seem very likely that she'd fight with a
boy. And a lot of girls would have done more than just
push her away if she'd pulled their hair the way she
did mine. Maybe she liked to fight. Maybe she'd been
trying to get me to fight with her that day in gym class.
She probably thought I was a real jerk not to get back
at her.

After school that night I helped Grandma make
supper. I peeled the potatoes while Grandma made
hamburger patties and cut up onions.

"I'm glad you kids are back now where you can eat
decent food, anyway," Grandma said, as she put the
big cast-iron frying pan onto the stove and turned on
the heat under it. The blue gas flame flared way up
around the sides of the pan, and then she turned it
down low. It was the same pan we'd had out at Lake
Lune; Grandma had scrubbed most of the rust off it.
She'd bought one of those big, flat aluminum covers at
the dime store, so it had a cover again.

I thought of the day we'd buried the broken glass

cover out at Lake Lune, the one Grandma had covered the pot roast with when she came for that supershort visit and left without even eating. Mother had said, "Your grandma would have a fit if she were here now and saw that we'd broken this. Good thing she isn't," as though it were a big joke. Diane said, "You leave my grandma alone." But when Mother asked, "Since when did you get so lovey-dovey about *her*?" Diane didn't answer, just threw some more dirt into the hole. We were in a hurry to get everything cleaned up before Marge, the local taxi driver, arrived and saw the mess.

"Try to get the eyes completely out, Merle," Grandma said, leaning over my shoulder. She pointed to the brown dots that didn't come off when I peeled.

"It's sort of hard to get them out without digging."

"So dig," she said. "Use the point of the potato peeler."

"Like this?"

"That's fine. You'll get the hang of it pretty soon." She turned back to the stove and started shaping hamburger patties out of the hunk of ground beef she'd taken out of the refrigerator.

"Ow!" I said.

She turned around again. "What's wrong?"

"I poked myself with the peeler."

"You've got to be more careful. That thing's sharp."

"I noticed that."

"Well, I'm sure you never learned to peel potatoes from your mother."

"So what?"

57

"I was just thinking about when she was your age. I worked longer days then—I needed the overtime— and I used to ask her to get supper started before I got home."

I put down the peeled potato and started another one.

"You'll have to rinse those off before you cook them, Merle."

"The boiling water will clean them."

She took the potatoes I'd already peeled and put them into the aluminum colander with the stars punched out. She swished it around under the cold-water faucet for a while.

"I suppose Mother didn't wash potatoes right, either?" I said.

Grandma turned down the heat under the boiling water. "Are you almost done there? We should put them all in at once."

"Here's the last one," I said. I walked over to the sink and rinsed it off.

Grandma was cutting the potatoes into quarters and tossing them into the boiling water. After all the potatoes were in, she put the cover on the pan, turned the heat down low, and then leaned against the sink. "I don't know if Elaine used to wash potatoes or not."

"Didn't you watch her? You sure watch me close enough."

"I'd come home from work, dead tired after a long day at the office, and the door would be locked. 'Let me in,' I'd say. 'Elaine, it's me, Mother.' She wouldn't

58

answer me, but I'd hear her in there, peeling potatoes."

"How could you hear her peel potatoes?"

"Well, you know what I mean. I'd hear her clattering around, running water into the pan, opening the refrigerator to get the potatoes out. So you see, she got her way after all."

"Her way?"

"Well, I stopped asking her to peel potatoes. I mean, my God, one day I spent twenty minutes out in the hall, trying to talk to Elaine through the door. You can imagine what the neighbors thought."

"But didn't you have a key?"

"Of course I had a key. But we lived in the city then, and everything had to be double and triple locked. She'd put the chain lock on, and I couldn't unlock *that* from the outside."

There was a hiss from the stove, as the potato water boiled over onto the burner. Grandma raced over and pulled the pan lid off until the boiling settled down again. Then she put the lid back on, but with a slight crack for the steam to escape. She always did this when she boiled potatoes, and they always boiled over. But she's a real energy freak; she always says boiling water in a pan without a lid is like burning dollar bills.

When we sat down at the table, Grandma said, "You know I have to go back to work tomorrow, don't you?"

We all nodded and kept chewing. Hamburgers with poppyseed rolls and fried onions and ketchup and A-1 sauce and mashed potatoes and carrot sticks were quite a meal compared to what we'd been used to at the end in Lake Lune. Oatmeal, oatmeal, oatmeal—food of horses and Carlsons.

"I'll write the number by the phone in case you need to call me after school for any reason. But I don't expect that you will."

"Okay," Ron said. "We'll be fine. We won't watch too much TV and we'll only make three batches of popcorn, and . . ."

"If I lose my job, I don't know what I'll do, Ron—what any of us will do. But I won't go to work tomorrow morning unless you all three promise to behave."

"Us?" Diane said, her eyes opening wide. Then she giggled and poured a little more ketchup on her hamburger.

"If only your grandpa were still alive," Grandma said. "I don't know what I'm going to do."

"Where have I heard that before?" Ron said. " 'He's not dead—he's just sleeping.' " Mother used to say that in Lake Lune.

"Make fun of me then," Grandma said. "After all, I don't have any feelings." She stood up and carried her plate into the kitchen. We could hear her dishing up ice cream as she talked. "You'd *think* after *all* I've *done* for you, you'd show a *little* apprecia tion." The ice cream must have been frozen hard. Every time she dipped into it she said her words harder.

"We *are*," Ron said. "Or at *least* we *try* to *be*."

Grandma came back with a tray. On it were four cut-glass bowls with ice cream and a cherry on top.

60

"What—no nuts?" Ron said.

"Keep it up," Grandma said. "Just keep it up."

"Keep what up?" he asked. "I ain't doin' nothin' nohow and I ain't plannin' to."

"I'm going to take a nap," Grandma said. "A ten-minute nap. I've had a long day. I'd like to see those dishes done before I wake up."

"That'll be a cute trick," Ron said. "Can you see in your sleep?"

Ron took the garbage out, and Diane and I did the dishes. First, though, Diane closed the kitchen door and turned on the radio. The newest song by the Carp came on:

Don't carp at me, 'cause I'm watching you,
Whatever you say, whatever you do.
This is a fishy tale, glub, glub.
But don't break my heart, I'm not a flub.
You're my very own fish, let me give you a kish,
We'll swim together—swish, swish, swish.

A stupider song it would be hard to find. Diane started making swimming motions, like the movements the Carp make when they perform this song on TV. There's a woman Carp—a Carpess?—who wiggles in and out among all the male Carp. She's the only one who doesn't have a guitar.

I handed Diane a dish towel. "Fish don't have hands," she said.

"Use your fins, then."

It didn't take long to do the dishes, but the pots and pans were something else. I hate scrubbing pots and pans, but I finally scrubbed all the grease out of the cast-iron frying pan and put the pan into the drainer for Diane to dry. I dumped out the dishwater, which was black from the frying pan, and bent under the sink for the cleanser to wash out the sink. When I stood up again, I noticed that Diane was drying the frying pan with the dish towel. "No, Diane! Use paper towels for that; the towel will get filthy."

But it already was streaked with black from the pan.

"How was I supposed to know?" She clanged the pan down onto the stove.

"Save the pieces!" Grandma said, as she walked through the kitchen door.

Diane grabbed the dish towel and put it behind her back.

"You kids did a great job," Grandma said. "And Ron took out the garbage, too? It sure is nice to have my helpers back."

"Nice to be back," Diane said, as she walked sideways out of the kitchen. I could hear her humming the Carp song as she ran upstairs to stuff the wet dish towel into the hamper at the head of the stairs. I didn't want to be around when Grandma discovered it, but maybe she wouldn't—there's always hope.

Diane was asleep by nine, and Ron and I went to bed at nine-thirty. I don't know whether he went right to sleep or not, but I read for a while. If I were Francie Nolan and some old-bag librarian recommended the very same book week after week, without looking up, I'd punch her in the mouth. After a while, I drifted off to sleep, the book still in my hands.

A loud thud woke me up again. The book had fallen on the floor. My light was still on, and I looked at the clock. Two o'clock. God, I'd be zonked for school the next day.

Even after I turned the light off, it was hard to go back to sleep, though. I had been dreaming of potato peelers and eyes—only in the dream they were the eyes of Mr. Sarow, and no matter how many times I dug them out, I couldn't make them stop looking at me. I finally dreamed they all had eyepatches on, and the next thing I knew, it was morning.

7

Eighth graders are mediocre at Bronwyn Junior High. I read somewhere that "mediocre" means middle, but of course it means other stuff, too—like crummy. The seventh graders are the babies of junior high, and the ninth graders think they're so smart—they're just about in high school. The eighth graders just plug along, being in the middle, and nobody pays much attention. Unless you belonged to one of the cliques—those kids thought they were really hot stuff.

One new clique called itself the "WBs." The rumor was that WB stood for "White Breast," but they only giggled if anyone asked them.

Everyone knew that Bronwyn means "white breast" in Welsh, but the school mascot was a white whale. In the introduction to the yearbook, one of the English teachers wrote that "according to some authorities, 'Bronwyn' means 'white beast.' " Those authorities must have been bad spellers. And in any case, since when are whales beasts?

But the WBs were something else again—now them, I could call beasts. My old best friend, Kayla, was in the group; she would hardly even say hello to me anymore. We had gone to elementary school together—all the way through, from first grade to sixth grade. So when we hit junior high, we hung around together in seventh grade. About four elementary schools all "fed" into good old White Whale Junior High, and in seventh grade people mostly stuck with their elementary-school friends.

But by the time I started back at Bronwyn in November, Kayla was busy hacking her hair off with fingernail scissors, streaking it orange and purple with food dye, and stuffing herself into too-small sweaters and too-short skirts. I recognized one outfit she used to wear in about fifth grade—who'd want to wear worn-out old baby clothes in junior high?

"You're just so out of it, Merle," Kayla said to me one day. "You were up there in the sticks too long or something. Get your act together."

We were walking home from school together, by accident. We used to walk home together every day in seventh grade, since we lived in the same direction, but now a lot of times Kayla went home with kids from other districts. Instead of walking west with me, she'd walk north, south, or east with them. I'd seen them leave a few times. They wore the strangest outfits—fake-leopard coats, black tights with red high heels, or rhinestone-studded orange harlequin glasses I wouldn't be caught dead in.

"You going to the dance Friday night?" Kayla asked.

"What dance?"

She stopped dead in the street.

"Kayla!" I said. "You'll get run over. Come on." I grabbed her elbow and pulled her over to the sidewalk. She kept staring at me.

Finally she said, " 'What dance?' Do I believe my ears?"

I just kept walking; I didn't answer her.

She caught up with me. "Everybody who is anybody knows about the dances at Westin Field."

"Oh, those dances."

"Have you ever gone?"

"Well, no, but I remember that last year people used to talk about them. . . ."

"Didn't you ever go last year? I did."

"My mother thought I was too young last year."

"What does she think this year?"

"I'll have to . . . ask her." I hadn't told Kayla about Mother yet.

"You still have to ask your mother if you can go pee-pee, too? Still mama's little baby girl, huh?"

I thought of Mother in some hospital up in Wisconsin, waiting for permission to be moved to a hospital closer to Bronwyn.

"Not exactly."

"Why're you frowning, Merle? Lighten up. Everybody'll be there Friday. Why don't you come?"

I thought of Ricky and the last dance I'd been to, in Lake Lune. I didn't think I was ready for that yet. "You'll probably go with the WBs, I suppose?"

"Well, of course," Kayla said. "Wouldn't you? *If* they asked you, I mean."

"Which they won't."

"Well, if you worked on yourself a little, Merle."

"I don't want to work on myself. I like myself fine."

"Well, I hope you're happy together. I mean, if you don't want any friends. . . ."

"I can find other friends," I said. "You're not the only person in the world, you know."

She yawned and then smiled at me. She had on bright orange lipstick, outlined in purple around the edges. "Suit yourself," she said. "But if you ever want to be popular in this school. . . ."

"I don't!" I said. "I have more important things to think about than being popular."

"Well, great," she said. "See ya later, Merle."

We'd come to the corner where we had to go in different directions. In seventh grade we used to stand and talk, sometimes for half an hour, before we'd say good-bye and walk home. Sometimes we'd go home with each other, too, and talk more there. Kayla's mother and father worked and my mother and grandmother worked, but we both had brothers and sisters at home, so we'd go into either her room or my room, depending on whose house we went to, and talk until supper time. We'd try on lipstick or nail polish. She had a tape deck, so we'd listen to tapes at her house. I had a radio, so at my house we'd listen to that. But we never tried an orange lipstick, or purple lipstick, either. We'd been into pale pink mostly.

"See you tomorrow, Kayla!" She was already half-way down the block, but she turned and waved. I watched for a while as she walked away from me, her white shrug a little grimy, her hair bleached blond with bright stripes of color. Kayla's shrug was fake lambswool. I looked down at my jacket. Beige cotton with a hood trimmed in fake fur that was just fuzzy, not an imitation of anything.

When I got home, Diane was sitting at the kitchen table, drinking chocolate milk and reading a book. There was chocolate powder all over the table. I poured myself some milk, mixed in some chocolate, and sat down at the table.

"How was school?" I asked Diane.

"Okay," she said. "They're doing different stuff from what we had in Lake Lune, though."

"I can help if you want," I said.

"Naw," she said, turning the page of the book. "It doesn't matter, anyway."

"Sure it does; it matters a lot."

She looked at me. "Maybe to you. Not to me."

"But it should matter to you. You need to study and go to college and . . ."

"I'm only nine," she pointed out. "Maybe there

won't even be any college by the time I'm old enough."

I thought of Kayla, telling me to work on myself so I could be a WB—whatever that was. "Sorry, Diane," I said. "I didn't mean to tell you what to do."

"That's good," she said.

"But if Mother were here, she'd—"

Diane slammed the book shut and stood up. "She's not here, and you're not her." She walked out of the kitchen and left the door swinging behind her.

Ron swung the door through the other way after a minute. "What's with Diane?" he said. "She's sitting in there hitting her fist against a book and saying, 'Merle's not my mother, Merle's not my mother.'"

"God only knows," I said. "Why don't you ask her?"

"Don't feel like it. Anything to eat?"

"Chocolate milk."

"That's it?"

"No, Ron—look for yourself. There's tons of stuff, but I'm not going to find it for you."

He put two pieces of bread into the toaster and took the peanut butter out of the cupboard. "God, is this a nice change from Lake Lune," he said.

"I guess," I said. "Sometimes I wish we were still there, though."

"Come on," he said. "That's ridiculous."

"I know. But the kids were nicer."

"What kids? I thought you and Kayla were blood sisters or something."

"Not anymore. Now she's a WB."

"What's that?"

"Oh, it's some stupid clique at Bronwyn Junior High. Wait till next year—you'll find out. They pass around slam books, and they . . ."

"What's a slam book?" He got out a jar of marshmallow cream and spread it on one piece of bread, then squished it together with the piece he'd spread with peanut butter.

"A slam book's a little notebook—the kind with wires at the top. Every page has a different person's name on it."

"So?"

"So then you pass it around and everybody writes on each page all the rotten things they can think of about that person."

"I can't wait," Ron said. "Sounds like a wonderful way to waste your life."

"Mostly just girls do it. They put boys' names in, though."

"How do you know about this, Merle?" he asked. He was licking marshmallow fluff off his fingers, one by one. "Don't tell me you've got one of these slam books."

"Only the WBs are allowed to have them."

"Says who?"

"Well, I don't know. That's what everybody says."

"Just ignore it," Ron said. He walked toward the door.

"Put your dishes in the sink," I said.

"Why?"

"Otherwise I have to, that's why—and I don't feel like it!"

"All right, all right. Don't be so touchy. What's with you, anyway?"

"Everything!" I said. "Everything, everything, everything."

"Could you be more specific?" Ron was laughing.

"No! I could not be more specific. I could not be more anything!"

8

"I just don't understand it," Grandma said at supper the next night.

"What don't you understand?" Ron asked, as he helped himself to more bread.

"What's going on around here."

"In what way?" he asked.

"In the way that all you kids do lately is bicker."

"So?"

"So is this the way you acted up at Lake Lune? Or are you doing it for my benefit?"

Nobody said anything.

"Well, I certainly hope you're going to act a little better than this when we go see the counselor."

It was the first we'd heard of any counselor since the day Ms. Pauley and Grandma had talked about family counseling the day we left Lake Lune.

"I'd be ashamed to take you if I thought you'd do nothing but bicker, the way you've been doing."

"Merle's not my mother!" Diane said.

"I never said I *was*." I slammed my milk glass down on the table so that milk sloshed out.

"This is what I mean," Grandma said. "I wish you'd try to be a little better tempered, Merle. You're the oldest, you know, and . . ."

"I've always been the oldest," I said. "I'm *sick* of being the oldest all the time."

"It's a little late to do anything about it now," Ron said.

"Besides, you get to be Mother's pet because you are the oldest," Diane said.

I thought of Mother and Mr. Sarow. "You are my oldest child, Merle," she had said. "I don't have anyone else."

"No!" I said. "No, no, no!"

"What's with you?" Ron asked, rocking back onto the back legs of his chair.

"Stop that!" Grandma said. "You'll break the chair."

He sat back upright again. "Okay, okay," he said. "Can I be excused?"

"*May* I?" I said.

"Will you just cool it?" he said. "I don't correct *your* grammar."

"Nothing to correct," I said.

"Doesn't anybody want any ice cream?" Grandma asked. "I bought chocolate sauce, too."

73

After we were done, Grandma said, "I'll do the dishes with Diane tonight, Merle. Why don't you go do your homework so you can get to bed early tonight. I think maybe you're overtired."

"Okay, I guess I'll go take a bath," I said.

I could hear Grandma and Diane talking as I walked toward the staircase. "Don't get so worked up, honey," I heard Grandma say. "Try to remember that she's older than you are and—"

"*You*'re not my mother, either," Diane said loudly. Then they lowered their voices so I couldn't hear.

Just as I reached the staircase Grandma called out, "Did I tell you Michele Dvorak called this afternoon, Merle?"

"No," I said, and went back to the kitchen. "What did she want?"

"She didn't say—just said to call her. I suppose she wants you to start baby-sitting again."

"I wonder how she knew I was back."

"I suppose she saw you walking to school or something."

"Is it okay for me to baby-sit if she asks?"

"Well, if you make it early on weeknights and get your homework done, that's fine. And I don't see why you can't baby-sit on the weekends."

"Thanks," I said, and picked up the phone. I had to put it down again and look up the Dvoraks' number, though; it had been months since I'd called them. Their little boy, Jason, was five, and when I'd last seen her, Michele Dvorak was pregnant. So they must have two kids by now—a new baby and a five-year-old.

"Dvoraks," she said, after the phone had rung a couple of times.

"Hi, Mrs. Dvorak. It's Merle Carlson."

"Merle! It's so good to hear your voice—it's been, what, four months or so?"

"Yeah—since July."

"No, we went on vacation at the end of June, remember? I haven't seen you since school let out last spring, I don't think. How are things?"

"Fine," I said. "I'm in eighth grade now."

"Have you dyed your hair purple yet?"

"No! Why?"

"Oh, Kayla's been over here baby-sitting quite a bit. Have you seen her since she cut her hair and dyed it?"

"Uh, yeah, I've seen her."

"She's such a pretty girl, it seems a shame. . . . Well, anyway, I was wondering if you'd like to baby-sit Saturday night?"

"Sure. I don't know much about babies, though, so you'll have to tell me what to do. Did you have a boy or a girl?"

Mrs. Dvorak cleared her throat.

"You didn't have twins, did you?"

"No, I didn't have twins—I didn't have anything."

"You didn't?"

"I had a late miscarriage, Merle. The baby died."

"Oh, Mrs. Dvorak, that's terrible. I'm so sorry."

"Thanks, Merle. I was pretty shook up about it, but I'm getting over it."

"Um, what time do you want me to come Saturday night?"

"Seven-thirty would be fine. Would you check and see if midnight would be too late to stay out? You can call me back."

"I'm sure midnight's fine," I said. "I used to baby-sit until midnight last year, remember?"

"Okay. Bring your books or something. Jason will be asleep by eight."

"Great. See you Saturday."

"Bye, Merle."

After I hung up the phone, I went into the bathroom. I closed the drain in the tub and turned on the hot and cold water. I put a capful of bubble bath into the water, and then two more capfuls. The bathroom started to steam up; it smelled like a fake pine forest. I went upstairs to my room to get my bathrobe on. As I walked up the stairs, I called out, "Anybody who wants to get in the bathroom, now's the time. I'm going to take a bath!"

"Whoop-de-doo," Ron said. He was at the top of the stairs when I got up there. "Big deal—so you're taking a bath."

I ignored him and went to my room and closed the door. I pulled up the surface of my pullout desk and scribbled some numbers on a piece of paper. If Mrs. Dvorak asked me to baby-sit once a week, and if I saved it all. . . . I started to make a list of things I could buy that I really needed: sewing machine, high leather boots, material for clothes, plus thread and stuff. The list was getting longer, and I was getting discouraged, when all of a sudden I heard Grandma's voice yelling up the stairs.

"Merle Carlson, you get down here this minute!" she said.

"Coming," I said. "Just a second." I took off my clothes and pulled on my robe. I was looking for my hairbrush when I heard Grandma climbing the stairs. "I *said* I was coming," I said. I ran out toward the stairs. I could see Grandma was really steamed.

"I thought you were a teenager," she said. "That should mean something."

"What are you talking about?" I said. "I just came upstairs to get the stuff I needed for my bath . . . my bath!" All of a sudden I remembered the water running and running and the bubbles. "Oh, my God!" I said. "My bath!"

"I've turned it off for you," she said. "But I didn't realize you were still a baby who needed help taking a bath."

"Kayla asked today if I still needed help going pee-pee," I said.

"Merle, what is your problem?" Grandma said. "I thought you were getting to be a grown-up girl, and here you are, acting like a kindergartner."

"I'm going to baby-sit for Jason Saturday night, so I can't be a kindergartner myself, can I?"

"Go take your bath," she said. "And try to pull yourself together a little."

There were bubbles up to the very rim of the tub.

I opened the drain, then hung my robe on the hook on the back of the bathroom door, and locked the lock. I put one toe into the tub, but all I could feel was bubbles until finally I got down to the water. I climbed into the tub, then slid in all the way to my shoulders while the water whoosed out the drain. When the water covered my ears, I turned on the hot-water tap with my foot. I could feel the porcelain all along the length of my body, my hips, bottom, and my whole back and shoulders. I could hear the water from the faucet hitting the water already in the tub, but the water around my ears muffled it. I closed my eyes.

If there's anything more relaxing than a hot, soaking bubble bath, I don't know what it is, but it still doesn't turn your brain off. "If you'd just do something with yourself," Kayla said. "Try to pull yourself together a little," Grandma said. "You are so out of it," Jinx said. I slithered around in the water, letting the bubbles move over me.

The bath was finally totally warm, and it was near the top again, so I turned the hot-water tap off. The water around my head felt like a liquid helmet. I swished my hair back and forth, and felt it swirling around my neck and my ears. It felt like thin wisps of cooked spaghetti or the tentacles of some soft underwater animal. How nice it would be just to feel things, like a jellyfish, and never have to think at all. Just sting things that get in your way, and swim along, your mouth open for food, your body one with the water. What a kick it would have been if my hair could have stung Jinx that day she pulled it, just reached out and hurt her when she touched it. I could have been cool as a cucumber, not even looked at her, just let my hair do the talking—*zap, zap*, like some electric protection fence. *Touch me, lady, you're dead. Fuck you—I don't even have to look at you to hurt you. Come near me and you'll be sorry. Even if I don't see you coming, I'm protected.*

After a while the water cooled down and I opened the drain with my big toe. The bathwater went spinning off down the drain, bubbles and all. I just lay there, feeling it slide away.

When all of the water was gone, the slimy porcelain tub felt hard, like it could bruise me if I moved too fast.

I stood up and pulled the shower curtain inside the tub and turned on the spray to get my hair clean. First shampoo, then creme rinse. Might as well be clean clear through. Squeaky, squeaky clean, squeaky Merle, the squeaky pearl.

By the time I was done rinsing my hair, my cheeks were red and my skin tingled. I dried off, opened the window a crack to let the steam escape, then put on my robe, wrapped my hair in a towel, and ran upstairs. I stretched out on the bed with the patchwork quilt over me, my heart beating fast from the hot water and the run upstairs.

The quilt was scratchy. It was some old ratty thing made of scraps from somebody's ragbag—pieces of fabric in all different sizes and colors and designs, all stitched together for warmth, if not beauty. It had been around since God was a baby, or at least since

Grandma was, and it looked like something the cat dragged in. Little tufts of yellow yarn held the layers together. The scratchy side was a blue-and-gray wool plaid. The other side was soft, but it wasn't even. It was made up of odd-shaped patches of different fabrics, with even some velvet thrown in. Right in the middle was a big, bright green square of satin that gave two names—Glenda and Karl—and their wedding date. They probably loved each other then—everybody seems to love each other at the beginning, before everything falls apart—and Glenda must have stitched up this quilt as a way to show that she knew that they'd always stick together, the way all the little pieces of the quilt did. The yarn was unraveling at the tips, though . . . and the scraps . . . were . . . getting more and more raggedy . . . like the odds and ends . . . from the ragbag they'd . . . started out in.

When Grandma came up to say goodnight, I was dozing. She woke me up, and I got ready for bed. The jaggedy lines of the quilt were pressed onto my cheek in a strange, red, crooked pattern, like I'd been sleeping so hard I'd became one with the bed. When I turned out the light, I had trouble sleeping at first. My heart was pounding fast, the way it does when you've been sleeping hard and then wake up.

The quilt felt so soft against my back, like a big, warm pillow. I realized I'd been dreaming. In the dream, Mother had said something to me. Mr. Sarow had been in it, too. He stood next to Mother, wearing a plaid jacket; Mother wore pajamas. Her hair was long and stringy, golden blond hair winding down to her feet. She had no shoes or slippers on. Her toenails were long and sharp and painted purple. "Only you can tell the truth, Merle," she said. Mr. Sarow bobbed and nodded, nodded and bobbed. "Only you, only you, only you."

I sat up in bed and smoothed out the quilt above me. I could feel the bumps where the pieces of yellow yarn that held the layers together were. I could feel the different fabric pieces on the crazy-quilt side—velvet, wool, satin, silk. Did Great-grandma Glenda know when she stitched all those pieces together that some-day her great-granddaughter would lie awake under the quilt, tossing and turning and worrying? When she sewed it, she probably didn't think twice about her own children, let alone her great-grandchildren. Prob-ably she was thinking about her new husband and what they'd do under the quilt.

And what they did was to have a bunch of kids who went and had a bunch of grandchildren. One of whom was, at this very moment, tossing and turning under some starched and scratchy sheets in a hospital some-where with a bunch of other crazy people, all hoping to get well soon so they could go home to their loving families.

Great-grandma Glenda couldn't possibly have known any of that. And yet she saw me when I was a baby, and she used to baby-sit for Mother. I was named after her. Merle Glenda. She was Glenda Merle.

Of course, I could have been named after Nancy Drew, too, and it wouldn't have made any difference to anybody, certainly not to Nancy Drew herself.

Nancy Drew Carlson. With a roadster all her own and a handsome, gallant father and a traincase in the trunk of the roadster at all times. In the traincase would be a toothbrush, a nightgown, and a swimsuit. Never know when you might need a swimsuit.

Funny, though, Nancy Drew didn't even have a mother—just her handsome lawyer father who gave her everything she wanted and thought she was super-perfect, no matter what she did. Of course, everything she did was the right thing to do, but still. . . .

It would be nice to do nothing but the right thing, and to have everybody around you know that you did everything right. It would be nice to be rich, too, and have relatives that you weren't ashamed of. It must be wrong to be ashamed of your family. Another thing that would be nice is if you could make yourself feel and think the things you were supposed to think and feel, instead of the crap that floats into your mind without so much as a by the way. Who knows where some of these thoughts come from—like the matted-down fluff that's hidden in the middle of a quilt. You never see it unless one of the two sides rips or falls apart, but it's the invisible middle that makes the quilt warm.

When I got to the Dvoraks' house on Saturday night, I couldn't help looking at Mrs. Dvorak's stomach. It didn't look any different than usual; it looked like anybody else's stomach. She had on a beautiful, bright blue dress that glittered when she walked. It looked like silk, but it was probably polyester. She wore high, high heels, black with tiny gold buckles and straps that crossed over her ankles. Her hair was black and cut so that it hung much longer in the back, with curly bangs in front. She had pulled her hair behind her ears; she wore long, dangly earrings that looked like iridescent feathers.

"We're going dancing!" she said. "It's been years, Merle—just years since we've been dancing."

"What's my better half saying?" Mr. Dvorak said, as he came into the living room buttoning his suit jacket.

"Don't believe a word she says—we go dancing all the time."

"Or at least we did ten years ago," she said.

"Average it out," he said.

Jason came over and grabbed my hand. "Will you read to me, Merle? Please?"

"Sure. Where are your books?"

He held up *The Cat in the Hat.*

"I must have read that to you twenty times, Jason. Aren't you sick of it by now?"

"It's still his favorite," Mrs. Dvorak said, shaking her head. "But you can find a different book in Jason's room if you want to."

"Oh, please, Merle—*The Cat in the Hat*. Please?"

"Sure," I said. "You want to read in your room?"

He tugged at my hand and leaned down the hall toward his room, so that I either had to move with him or fall over. "Well, good night," I said, as I started down the hall.

"The phone number's on the phone, Merle," Mrs. Dvorak said. "And help yourself to milk or whatever."

I heard them closing and locking the front door as I followed Jason to his room.

"I have a night-bright now," he said, pointing to a little purple plastic elf. "See?" He turned off the light switch, and the elf glowed.

"I think it's called a night-light," I said.

"Uh-uh. It's *mine,* and I call it a night-bright."

I read him *The Cat in the Hat,* and then *Angus and the*

Cat. I don't know why nobody ever writes kids' books about gerbils or horses.

"Okay, kiddo, I'll sing you a song if you hop into bed."

"Oh, Merle, do I hafta? I didn't even brush my teeth yet."

"Well, go brush your teeth then."

He hopped down off the bed and padded along the hallway to the bathroom. He had on dark green pajama sleepers with white plastic feet, so he swished as he walked. By the time I got to the bathroom, he was standing on a stool he'd pulled up to the sink. He had a little white toothbrush in one hand, and he was squeezing the toothpaste tube with the other. He had about three layers of multicolored toothpaste gel on the brush by the time I realized what he was doing.

"No! Jason—that's too much toothpaste."

"My mommy lets me."

"But it's wasteful."

"Okay. You can put some back in."

He handed me the toothpaste tube and started to give me the toothbrush.

"Just brush," I said. "You can't get toothpaste back into the tube, you know."

"You can't?" he said, opening his eyes wide. "Oh." He opened his mouth and stared at himself in the bathroom mirror as he brushed his teeth. He leaned close to the mirror and got toothpaste on the glass.

After a while, he stopped brushing, hung his toothbrush up in the metal holder, and rinsed his mouth out with water. Then he climbed down from the stool.

I handed him a blue washcloth. "You'd better wash your face," I said. "You've got toothpaste all over your mouth."

He laughed. "That's my daddy's washcloth!"

"Oh, well, is this one yours?"

"I don't have a washcloth."

"Well, you can't go to sleep like that. You'll get toothpaste all over your pillow."

"I don't care."

"Your friends will call you 'toothpaste breath.' "

He laughed. "They will?"

I grabbed the nearest towel and wet the corner of it with cold water. I rubbed it around his mouth until the toothpaste was gone, then dried off his mouth with the other end of the towel.

"Well, time for bed."

"What about my song?"

"Not until you're *in* bed with the lights out, and the covers are pulled up to your chin."

He ran down the hall, and I could hear him jump onto his bed. When I got to his room, all I could see on the bed was a big hill of covers.

I put my hands on the bedclothes. "It's a monster! Oh, no, a monster has eaten Jason!"

The bedclothes shook, and I heard Jason giggling.

"The monster's laughing! Oh, what can I tell Jason's mommy?"

He poked his head up from under the covers. "Here I am! Merle—tell her I'm okay!"

I pretended I couldn't see him. "Jason? Do I hear Jason talking?"

"Merle! I'm right here!"

I turned around the other way. "Right where?"

"Here."

"Your mommy will be so worried when I tell her about the monster."

Jason jumped onto my shoulders. "I'm here! I'm here! I'm not lost—don't tell my mommy I'm lost. I'm right here. See?"

"Well, no, I can't see you—but I can hear you!" His hands were over my eyes.

"Don't scare my mommy, Merle. Please?"

"Oh, Jason, she'll know it's just a joke. My mother used to play the same game with me when I was a little kid."

"Does she anymore?"

"No."

"Why not? Are you too old or something?"

"Yeah, I'm too old or something."

"Sing!"

First I sang him the Carp's fish song. When I got to the part that goes: *You're my very own fish, let me give you a kish,* Jason started giggling. "A kish! A kish! Don't you mean a kiss?"

"Doesn't rhyme. This kind of a song has to have a rhyme."

He started giggling. "Sing it again! Sing it again, Merle!"

"Nope—time for lights out!" I pulled the covers up around his ears, turned out the overhead light, and said good night as I closed his door.

" 'Night, Merle." I could hear him yawning and moving around a little, but more and more slowly.

When I got back to the living room, I grabbed the *TV Guide* off the top of the television set and looked to see what was playing. Not much. Too bad the Dvoraks didn't have cable, like Kayla did. I used to go over to her house sometimes and watch it. We even watched a couple of dirty movies until her mother found about out about it and bought a black box.

Nothing much on TV on a Saturday night—an old war movie. A singing talent show. A rerun about a family with a bunch of kids who were happy all the time. "The Jolly Jensens," it was called. I turned it on. There was Jenny Jensen, trying to sneak a dog into her room without her mother seeing. It was the kind of dippy show where everybody walks around saying things like, "Oh, excuse me, it's all my fault," and giving each other little pats and putting sappy notes in lunchboxes.

Jenny's mother was not pleased when she found out about the dog. "You've got a dog in your bed?" she said. "You'll get bedbugs!" Jenny's sad face was on the screen as they broke away for commercials.

When the Jolly Jensens came back on, the father had thought of a solution. "We'll build a doghouse," he said jollily. So they all chipped in to build a doghouse. One kid held the nails, another kid had the hammer, a third had the dog on a leash. It went like that until they had built the dog a mini-mansion, with JOLLY painted on the door. They renamed the dog Jolly, so everyone would know he wasn't a mutt anymore—he was a Jensen.

There were some more commercials, and then the grand finale—a big birthday party for the dog, complete with paper streamers and party hats. "Since we don't know when his birthday is, we'll just have to give him one," Jenny Jensen said.

"How sweet," said her mother.

Barf me out—their damn dog lived better than a whole lot of people I knew.

10

Jinx couldn't play basketball anymore. With her eye-patch on, she couldn't see well enough to play. Besides, I think Ms. Garland was afraid she'd get even more hurt if she fell or ran into somebody or something.

Day after day, Jinx sat on the sidelines and watched the rest of us play. Her good eye would follow us back and forth; every time I glanced her way I saw her watching. She never brought a book or looked at anything but the basketball and whoever had it.

"The tournament is a week from Friday, girls," Ms. Garland said one day. "We'll number off for the playoff. . . ." There were groans from about half the class. "I think that will be a good end to our basketball unit. It's time to go on to volleyball." There were groans from the other half of the class. We were all sitting around on the gym floor, listening to Ms. Garland explain the rules. Jinx had the basketball in her lap; somebody must have handed it to her when the game ended. She was sitting cross-legged, with her arms around the basketball as though she were its mother. Her chin was resting on the orange rubber ball; I thought at any minute she'd move her chin toward her chest and give the ball a little kiss. She looked real weird, all hunched over the basketball like that, with her eyepatch and her long black sweater sleeves. She was dressed like she lived in a park or something. You'd think someone would have noticed what she looked like when she left for school in the morning. For some reason, I thought back to Lake Lune and my two school outfits. I had to thank my lucky stars there hadn't been any gym class there—God only knows what I would have done for gym clothes.

". . . Carlson?"

I looked up with a start. The whole class and Ms. Garland were all staring at me. I'd been looking so hard at Jinx I'd lost track of what was going on.

"Do *you* want the basketball, Merle?" Ms. Carlson asked. "We do have others, if you want one so badly."

"Oh—no—that's okay—I don't even like basketball too much. . . . I mean . . ."

"You don't have to like basketball to learn the rules," she said.

"And you don't have to learn the rules to like it," someone said, glancing over at Jinx.

"Written test a week from Thursday, girls!" Ms. Garland said. "And the playoff's a week from Friday. Your grade will be an average of how well your team does and how you do on the written test."

"Boy, am I in trouble," I said to Peggy, as we walked up to the showers. "Studying the rules won't be hard, but I can't learn to be coordinated between now and next Friday."

"At least you can play," a voice said behind us.

I turned around. Jinx was walking through the locker room just behind us. She must have been getting her bag and books from her locker.

"Maybe your eye . . ." I said.

"Maybe," she said. "But then he'll just . . ."

"Who?" Peggy said.

"None of your business," Jinx said, grabbing for her combination lock and twirling it.

When we got out of earshot, I looked at Peggy and Peggy looked at me. "Does she have a boyfriend?" Peggy said.

"I don't know," I said. "I just figured she'd had an accident."

"Well, she must have, but then why did she say? . . ."

"Beats me," I said.

When I started to get undressed to take my shower, though, I forgot about Jinx and her problems. There, on my underpants, was a bright spot of red. It had started again. I couldn't believe it. I just stared and stared at that little red spot. I would be able to have babies, after all. I wasn't under some kind of a curse —except the kind all girls get. I could be a mother someday, and I could get married like everybody else. I wasn't a freak. Mother's life and her Mr. Sarow and all the other stuff I could live with, as long as I was a normal person myself.

"Peggy!" I yelled. "The shower's all yours! I got my period!"

"Well, you don't have to sound so happy," she said. "Why, haven't you ever had it before or something?"

But I was already halfway out of the shower stalls. "Forget it," I said, as I half ran toward the stairs. When I got back down to the locker room, I walked as fast as I could to Ms. Garland's office. "Ms. Garland!" I said. "I need a pass. My period started and I have to go get—"

Ms. Garland was sitting in a chair behind her desk; she stared at me and then looked across her desk toward the other chair. There sat Jinx, slouched down into the chair with her feet stretched way out under the desk.

"Oh, excuse me," I said, starting to back out. "I didn't know—I didn't mean—I just—"

"It's okay, Merle," Ms. Garland said, reaching into her bottom drawer and taking out a blue paper package. "I keep these here for emergencies like this. Take a couple and bring back the rest of the package."

"Thank you," I said. I grabbed for the box and left without looking at Jinx.

"Close the door behind you, please," Ms. Garland

said. "I should have done that before."

As I closed the door, I heard her say to Jinx, "This must stop. I've got to tell someone. You can't go on like this."

But as she spoke, I heard Jinx saying softly, over and over again, "No, no, no, no. He'll kill me."

God—whatever Jinx was into was pretty heavy duty. Whatever she'd gotten herself into was more than she could deal with—that was for sure.

As I walked into the john, all I could think about was that now I could have a baby, and no one could stop me. Not even my mother with her evil eye. She could stare at me all she wanted and my body was going to work right, anyway. She couldn't stop it. She wasn't in charge of what happened to me. I didn't have to be weird just because she was.

Of course, now I got to go back to the good old days of worrying about stained clothes and stained sheets and buying Kotex and all that stuff. No wonder they call it the curse. I read once that natives use leaves; they have to go hide in the bushes when *it* comes every month. In America we're much more civilized—we just pretend it doesn't exist at all. Half the women in America probably menstruate, and it lasts for a week once a month, so—what did that make it?—half the women are a quarter of the population and a quarter of them—one-sixteenth of the entire population of the United States has its period at any given time. But you'd never know it to look at them. Everyone keeps mum about it, except when "emergencies" happen.

I was never so glad in my life to be in an emergency.

When I got back to the locker room, Marlene was taking the bread bags off her hair. She unwrapped first one and then the other and carefully shook them out and folded them into her locker basket on top of her shower cap.

"Do you always use those?" I asked her.

"I have band next hour," she said. "I can't go there with wet hair, and this school's too cheap to provide hair dryers."

"Well, they'd understand if you were late, wouldn't they?"

"Two tardies and they drop you," she said. She was throwing her clothes on as fast as she could.

Good thing I wasn't in the band; I'd never make it there on time. I pulled on my tights slowly and tried to feel if I had cramps. I couldn't feel a thing more than a sort of downward pull, like bathwater swirling slowly out of a tub with a stopped-up drain.

11

When I got home from school there was a letter on the dining-room table. It was addressed to me, in pencil. I recognized Mother's handwriting, but it was all crooked. The sloppy lines of the address wandered down the envelope toward the corner, so that there was barely room for the zip code. Mother never used a pencil. She always said she got plenty of that in her work as a bookkeeper and on her own time she'd use a pen, thank you.

Her own time. Was this her own time, in the hospital? She wasn't working at a job. But probably they told her what to do a lot. Why would she use an unsharpened pencil, though, so that the lines were fat and hard to read? Maybe it was all they had. Or maybe they weren't allowed to use regular pens and pencils. Like those fat crayons kindergartners have to use until they get the hang of regular skinny crayons.

I went into the kitchen and put some milk in a pan for cocoa. I got out the marshmallows and some cups and spoons, then stirred chocolate milk powder into the milk until it turned the color of a Hershey bar. Ron and Diane would be mad I'd made it that dark. They liked it lighter, with lots of marshmallows. I hadn't meant to put in so much chocolate powder— just kept scooping the spoon in, tipping it over, scooping it in again.

When it was lukewarm, I poured myself a cup and sat down at the table to drink it. I stared at the envelope from Mother. The clock on the kitchen wall buzzed along. It was a round, blue plastic clock with white numbers; the electric cord hung down below it to the outlet. The gas fumes from the stove had turned the cord all yellow; dust seemed to cling to it, too, as if it were magnetic. The numbers on the clock were bright white, though; Grandma unplugged the clock every once in a while, took it down from the wall, and gave it a good scrubbing. But for some reason she never scrubbed the cord and every year it got yellower.

"We're home!" Ron and Diane called from the front door. They came racing in, their coats and boots still on. Their cheeks were red, and they were covered with snow.

"We were having a snowball fight," Diane said. "You know that big, fat bully, George?"

"You mean Georgie-Porgie?" I asked.

"Yeah, that's the one. Well, I got him right in the face with an ice ball!" She laughed. "You should have seen it—he started to cry and everything."

"Good thing I was there," Ron said. "God, was he mad!" He ladled out a cup of cocoa and plopped in some marshmallows.

"I can take care of myself," Diane said. She picked up the ladle.

"Hey, take your coats and boots off first," I said.

"Okay, okay," Ron said.

They took off their jackets, scarves, hats, boots, and mittens, and piled them onto the boot tray in the corner of the back hall.

"Hang up the jackets," I said.

"Aye-aye, sir . . . ma'am," Diane said.

When they were sitting at the table, too, drinking cocoa, I pointed to the envelope.

"Look what came today," I said.

"A letter from Mommy?" Diane said. "What's it say?"

"I don't know. I didn't open it yet."

"I'll open it for you," Diane said.

"No, that's okay." I opened it quickly. It was written on a piece of lined paper torn from a notebook, with the left-hand edges still ragged.

Dearest Merle, Ronald, and Diane,
    It's morning here, so you must be in school. The sky is dark now, but it could brighten up. It could also keep snowing, easily.

I wonder how your weather's been? Sunday we had turkey. Usually we have mystery meat, so it was a change.

I hope I'll be home for Christmas. I miss the three of you so much and, of course, your grandma, too. Please tell her I said so.

And write to me. I never get any mail.

Brush your teeth. All three of you.

Hugs, kisses, and love,
Your everloving mother

I picked up my book bag and started toward the stairs.

"Don't we get to read it?" Diane said.

I handed her the letter and the envelope. "Sure, you can read it."

"I don't know why nobody ever writes to us," Diane said.

"Your name's right here on the letter," I said. "Okay?" I put down my book bag and picked up the letter.

"But it wasn't on the envelope," she said. "See?"

"I can't help that," I said. "I didn't write the damn letter."

I grabbed my book bag and ran toward the staircase. There was a door at the foot of the stairs; I slammed it shut behind me. At the top of the stairs I stopped to get my eyes accustomed to the light before I went any farther. The upstairs was a big, partially finished attic, divided into three alcoves. The only one with a door was the big room in the middle, at the far end of the attic. Ron had the alcove to the right facing the big room and Diane had the alcove to the left. I had the regular room. All the shades in the upstairs were still drawn, so that the light was hazy and yellowish brown. I pulled up the shade above the staircase and then walked through Ron's area and pulled up his shade. Then I pulled up the shade in Diane's area and then the shade in my room. I closed the door and lay down on my bed. The light from the snow on the roof outside the window reflected all over the walls of the room. They were painted a deep bluish green, and the snow light made them look iridescent. I closed my eyes and kicked off my shoes.

I could feel the quilt underneath me, soft and pillowy. Grandma's mother had been a seamstress for other people, and after she got married she used all the scraps of velvet and silk left over from rich people's dresses and sewed them into a beautiful design. I always kept the blue-and-gray wool plaid side up, so the good side wouldn't get worn out.

Besides, it made me sad to look at all those tiny stitches and think of those dead people who were my great-grandparents. I never even knew them. It must be strange to have kids and then later they have kids and then they have kids. All these people coming out of each other, and who knows what's going to happen to any of them. Sometimes they'll be happy and sometimes they won't, but they all start out as little soft, cuddly worms. Even the ones who die before they're born, like poor Mrs. Dvorak's dead baby, who never got to be anybody's child or grandchild.

"You stay out of my room, Merle Carlson!" I looked up. Diane stood in the doorway and yelled at me. "Just because my room doesn't have a door doesn't mean you can just go in there any old time. . . ."

"Aw, Diane, all I did was pull up your shade, so it wouldn't be so dark up here."

"You have your own window and your own shade and your own room. Leave mine alone!" She slammed the door shut.

"All right," I said, and turned over onto my side. I could see Diane's point perfectly well. It just didn't seem worth arguing over. Nothing seemed worth arguing over. There had to be something else in life besides arguing and dying.

I must have fallen asleep briefly, because when I opened my eyes again the room was pink. The sun was setting and the light reflected in through my window. I stood up and leaned against the windowsill for a minute. The roof was very steeply slanted at different angles, so that the snow could slide off easily. An old pine tree grew crookedly up from the front yard toward my window. Whenever there was a heavy snow, Grandma always called the landlady, Mrs. Kingston, and said, "I'm warning you, that tree's going to fall and crush your house. . . . I just want you to know that you may lose your whole investment." I think Grandma was more worried about losing us, and I never heard Mrs. Kingston's end of the conversation, but the tree stayed there year after year, getting more gnarled and leaning closer and closer to the house, as if for warmth.

When we were little, we used to play with the sap that flowed from the pine tree. It was thick and amber colored and sticky. It oozed out in thick drips in the spring. We'd roll the sap around in our fingers, trying to make it into something, but it always got black and stuck to everything else instead of to itself. The smell was amazing—like something you'd use to wash the floor.

The tree was covered with snow now, though, and I figured Grandma must be due for her yearly call to Mrs. Kingston.

When I got downstairs, Diane was standing at the stove, stirring pudding, and Grandma was setting the table.

"Where've you been?" Grandma asked. "I've been home for an hour."

"I guess I fell asleep," I said.

"Must be nice," she said. "Go tell Ron it's time for supper, will you?"

I noticed Mother's letter lying upside down on the buffet. I put it in my pants pocket and went to call Ron.

"Mother thinks she's coming home for Christmas," I said to Grandma that night at supper. We were having meatza pizza and salad and pudding. I stared at the red pimiento piece in the middle of a sliced green olive. It looked like a weird Christmas decoration.

"First I've heard of it," Grandma said.

"We got a letter today."

"Who from?" Grandma's voice was sharp, like she was afraid of the answer.

"Mother."

"Oh, her."

"Who'd you think?"

"Well, I thought maybe the hospital, or. . . . You wouldn't open a letter addressed to me, would you? Not without my permission?"

"No," I said. "Why would I do that? It had my name right on it."

"I just meant if a letter came from one of the . . . doctors or the hospital or something."

"No," I said.

"Well, what else did she say?"

"Oh, that she misses you."

Grandma choked a little. "She *misses* me?"

"Well, I don't know. She said she did. You want to read it for yourself?"

"It's your letter."

"I don't mind. I'll go get it."

She read it quickly and then carefully refolded it. She slipped it back into the envelope as though it were a pair of panty hose she didn't want to snag.

"I think it's sad Mommy has to eat mystery meat," Diane said.

"Oh, boo-hoo," Ron said. "You think everything's sad."

"No, I don't," Diane said. "But she must be lonely . . . you can see she says she misses us."

"She says a lot of things," Grandma said, "not all of them true."

"What's the point of saying that?" I said.

"Have a little more pizza," she said to Ron.

"Sure," he said.

"Can she come home for Christmas?" I asked.

"It's not up to me."

"She thinks it is."

"Well, she's wrong," Grandma said, very quietly but firmly.

"Okay, okay, you don't have to get mad about it."

"I'm not mad," she said. "I didn't raise my voice."

"You know what I mean," I said. "You were yelling at me quietly."

Ron and Diane snickered.

"What's so funny?" I said. "Quit it."

They poked each other and laughed out loud.

"Cut it out!" I said. "Grandma, make them cut it out."

Grandma was stacking the plates. She used a fork to scrape the scraps off into the vegetable bowl. "I can't seem to make anybody do anything," she said. "Did the three of you act like this in Lake Lune, too?"

Nobody said anything. "I asked you a question," she said. "Did you? Or were you saving this kind of behavior for me?"

"That's ridiculous, Grandma," I said. "We didn't even know if we'd ever see you again when we were in Lake Lune."

She looked at me, the fork halfway down the last plate.

"I mean . . ." I said. "Well, you know how Mother talks when she. . . ."

Grandma finished scraping off the plate. She carried the stack of plates over to the sink, put them into the dishpan, and then turned on the hot water. "Damn," she said.

"What's wrong?" Diane said.

"Never mind," Grandma said. She turned the faucet off, hard. When she turned around, the front of her sweater was all wet.

"Oh, you squirted water on your clothes," I said.

"Merle, the Seeing-Eye dog," Ron said.

Grandma opened the refrigerator door and took out four custard cups. She put one in front of each of our places. Inside was chocolate pudding with maraschino cherries and coconut mixed in.

"Good pudding," I said, scraping the last of mine out.

"Don't hurt yourself," Grandma said. She ate slowly, a quarter-teaspoonful at a time. We had a rule that no one could leave the table until everyone was through. Ron, Diane, and I sat there, scraping out our empty pudding bowls while Grandma ate those little teases of pudding. All of our eyes looked at the tan Formica-covered table, and the pink-and-green flowered wallpaper. Finally Diane said, "They're dying."

"I wouldn't be a bit surprised," Grandma said.

Ron and I looked at each other. "Who's dying?" Ron asked.

Diane pointed to the window. There, on the sill, were six small African violets—pink, purple, magenta, white, lilac, and pale green. "They look fine to me," I said. I stood up and walked over to them.

"I'm not finished eating yet," Grandma said.

"Whoops!" I said. I sat back down at my place again. "The violets look fine to me."

106

"They would," Diane said.

"Well, what's wrong with them?"

"They're dying, stupid," Diane said. "That's what I've been trying to say." She stood up and walked over to the violets. "See, the flowers are falling off, and. . . ."

"Supper is not over yet, Diane," Grandma said. "Show a little respect."

"I *am* showing respect," she said, pulling a dead violet off. "I'm showing respect for living things. See?" She held up a brittle, papery, lilac-colored flower. Its tiny yellow center disappeared as she crumpled it between her fingers.

"You're getting flower dust all over the floor," Grandma said. "But what should you care? It's not your floor. I saw how you lived in Lake Lune when I wasn't around. The floor was so filthy I wouldn't—"

"Mother was sick," Diane said, stomping back to the table and leaning her hands hard on it. "She didn't know what she was doing."

"Is that your excuse?" Grandma said. "That you don't know what you're doing, either?"

"What a stupid thing to say," Diane said. "I didn't say that. . . . I was just trying to fix the flowers."

"Sounds like the name of a bad song," Ron said. He crooned: "*If only I could fix the flowers, if only I could make them bloom, maybe I could fix our love, and you'd come back to me soon. . . .*" His voice cracked.

I laughed.

"Very funny," Diane said. "You should go into

107

show business, so you could laugh at people all the time."

"That's not quite how it works," Ron said. "See, in show business, you get people to laugh at *you.* . . ."

"That would be even better," Diane said. "I'll come and laugh at you. I'd love to laugh at you—you're so *stupid!*" She sat down hard and glared at Ron.

"Laugh *with,*" Ron said. "You get the audience to laugh with you."

"That's not what you said," Diane said. "I wouldn't have said it if you hadn't said it."

"I just hope you're planning to sweep up the mess you made," Grandma said.

Diane jumped up from the table.

"Not now!" Grandma said. "When supper's over."

"But you said—" Diane said. "You just said to sweep up."

"Having a little trouble understanding what people say these days?" Ron asked. "Here, read my lips." He mouthed some words at her.

"Cut it out!" Diane yelled. "Just cut it out! You stop that!" She walked over to Ron.

"You're the one who should stop it," Grandma said. "You're acting like a kindergarten baby or something."

"I am not!" Diane said. "You know perfectly well I'm in fourth grade, and I'm not a baby."

"Well, act your age then," Grandma said.

"Act yours," Diane said.

"What did you say to me?" Grandma asked. "Did I hear you right?"

"Everybody in this family's going deaf," Ron whispered to me.

"I wouldn't mind," I whispered back. "Who wants to listen to this."

When we looked up from our whispering, though, it might have been better to have temporary blindness. There was Grandma, grabbing Diane by the arm. And there was Diane, trying to get her to let go.

"Oh, no, you don't," Grandma said. "You're going to your room."

"I'm running away," Diane said. "I'm never coming back."

"And just where will you go?" Grandma asked. She dropped Diane's arm, though, and walked over to put the coffeepot back on the burner. The blue flame flared up around the edges of the aluminum coffeepot, and then settled down to a blue glow below it.

"Anywhere!" Diane said. "Anywhere's better than this prison!"

"This isn't a prison, Diane," I said.

"What do you know about it?" she asked. "Just because you're everybody's little pet. You get to see Mother and we don't and. . . ."

"Everybody gets to see her pretty soon," Grandma said. "They can't seem to come up with a family counselor for us, but they're johnny-on-the-spot to send Elaine home as quick as they can."

That shut everybody up for a minute.

"Is she well?" Ron finally asked.

"Of course she's not well," Grandma said. "But all these fancy-dancy doctors who don't have to live with her think it's best that she not spend too much time in the hospital without *home visits.*"

She said home visits as though she were translating from a foreign language.

"Home visits?" Diane said. "You mean, we get to see her?"

"I guess so," Grandma said. "Unless, of course, you've run away in the meantime. Then I don't know when you'll ever get to see her."

"I was just kidding," Diane said, rubbing the toe of her sneaker against the kitchen floor. She was staring at the line the sneaker streaked across the linoleum.

"Look at me when you speak," Grandma said. "Quit marking up the floor. This is my house, and—"

"We rent," Diane said, looking Grandma straight in the face.

" 'We' don't do anything," Grandma said. "*I* pay the rent on this house, all by myself."

"Mother . . ." Ron said.

"Leave her out of this," Grandma said. "She doesn't pay the rent when she *is* here, and she sure as hell doesn't pay it when she's not."

"It's not her fault," Diane said. "She can't help it if she's sick."

"She can't help it she was born, either," Grandma

said. "She's always reminding me of that—I don't need you taking her side, too."

"Somebody has to," I said.

"Why?" Grandma said. "Why does everybody have to take her side all the time? You were there—you saw what happened in that courtroom. She is wrong sometimes, you know."

"She's right sometimes, too," I said. "Just because everybody's afraid of you doesn't mean you're always right."

Grandma walked over to the sink and began to do the dishes loudly. The three of us sat at the table, looking at the napkin holder in the middle. It was a blue plastic butterfly—really two plastic butterflies—connected at the bottom by a flat plastic piece. The paper napkins went in the middle, and usually they flopped over to one side or the other. All of a sudden Diane grabbed the butterfly holder and snapped it in two. Blue plastic flew everywhere.

"Ow!" Grandma said, putting her hand up to her neck, where the plastic had hit her. "What was that?" Soap dripped down her arm from her wet hands.

Diane threw what was left of the butterflies onto the floor and ran out of the room.

"I'm getting out of here," Ron whispered. He sneaked out the back door and I heard it close quietly as Grandma said, "Jesus H. Christ. What is wrong with you three? Ever since you got back from Lake Lune . . ."

She wasn't looking at me, but I didn't want to make her notice me by leaving the room. So I walked over to the windowsill and looked at the African violets for a while.

They were all covered with flowers. Some of the flowers were faded or brittle, but you could still see that they were trying to bloom. But there was one plant that didn't have a single blossom. It was on a shelf away from the window. Its leaves had curled up into themselves, and the whole plant looked as though it were trying to move itself over to the window. Its roots were even straining to get out of the soil on the side farthest from the light. It was only a stupid plant, without even any legs, but at least it knew what it wanted. It came right out and leaned—hard—toward the light.

I turned around and watched Grandma washing off the stove. Then I bent down and picked up the pieces of violet Diane had dropped. Lying on the floor like that, they looked like toenail clippings or something equally junky. You'd never know they'd been attached to real live plants, or that they'd been pretty. While I was at it, I grabbed the pieces of blue plastic that I could reach. I wasn't going to go crawling around behind Grandma, feeling the kitchen floor for broken plastic. Grandma's kitchen floor was always spotless, but still . . .

The kitchen floor that last morning in Lake Lune was covered with newspapers. "They've come for me!" Mother said when the police came. For once her paranoia was right on target, but maybe she wasn't entirely sorry they'd come for her. Maybe she was just a little bit glad that someone cared enough about her to remember she was there. And Mother must be more comfortable in the hospital—no matter what it was like—than in a dirty kitchen with newspapers all over the floor. Or out in the snow in her bare feet.

Mother always seemed to know what she didn't want, but she never had a very clear idea of what she did want. How can you get something if you don't even know what it is you want?

"You want to start drinking coffee?" Grandma said at breakfast Saturday morning. "What on earth for?"

"I want to grow up," I said.

"She wants to stay awake," Ron said.

I glared at him.

"Social error! Social error!" he said. "Excu-u-u-u-se me!"

I took a mug from the cupboard and poured coffee into it.

"Maybe coffee will make Merle wake up," Ron said to Grandma as I took a sip.

"Merle's awake," Diane said, as she walked into the kitchen rubbing her eyes. "See, she's right there— *drinking coffee?*"

"You'd think I were mainlining dope," I said. "I'm almost fourteen—that's old enough to drink coffee."

"My mother left school at fourteen," Grandma said. "She graduated from the eighth grade and went to work to help out her family."

"Your mother was a high-school dropout?" Ron said. "I'd keep that quiet if I were you."

"Watch your mouth," Grandma said. "She never started high school, so she never dropped out, either. Lots of people left school after eighth grade in those days."

"Merle, why don't you do that?" Ron asked. "You'd have more time for your beauty sleep."

"I said, *in those days,*" Grandma said. "Now people graduate from high school and go on to college. Times change."

"Could your mother read?" Diane asked.

"Can Merle read?" Ron asked. "What a stupid question."

"Oh," Diane said.

"She could write, too," I said. "Did you ever see the quilt on my bed? She embroidered her name and her husband's name and the date on it."

"Maybe she traced it," Diane said. "I used to do that, before I could really write."

"My mother knew how to read *and* write," Grandma said. "Plus she was a wonderful cook."

"How can you drink this stuff?" I asked Grandma, as she got up to pour herself another cup of coffee. "It's so bitter."

"I didn't think you'd like it," she said. "Pour some milk in—that should help a little."

I poured milk in almost up to the top, and it did cut the bitterness some.

"I'm about to go to the store," Grandma said. "Anything you need?"

"I don't think so," I said.

"You sure you don't need—you know—" She gave me a long stare.

"I have my own money now," I said. "I can pick up things I need myself."

"Oh, but I'm going to the store, anyway," she said. "I'll be glad to—"

"*No!*" I said. "Just leave me alone, will you?" I got up, poured more coffee in the cup, added more milk, and took the mug with me up to my room.

I sat down at my desk in front of the window. Most of the snow had melted off the pine tree, and it hadn't toppled the house down yet. I sipped the coffee slowly and looked out at the sidewalk below the tree's branches. My friend Theresa and I used to play hopscotch on that part of the sidewalk when we were little. That was before Theresa moved to the ritzy suburb three suburbs down from ours. I used to go and visit her sometimes and stay overnight, all through seventh grade. She moved away after sixth. I'd been meaning to call her ever since we'd gotten back from Lake Lune, but I hadn't gotten around to it.

When I looked out at the sidewalk, I could almost see Theresa out there, her short blond hair bobbing up and down as she jumped the hopscotch squares. She was always much more coordinated than I was, and she'd do those hopscotch squares in nothing flat. Toss the little stone, *hop*. Toss it again, *hop, hop*. Toss it again, *hop, hop, hop*. She was so skinny and she hopped so well, and now she lived in a ritzy suburb and had ten pairs of wool knee socks and a pink telephone in her bedroom. At least, she'd had all those things last year.

I sipped at the coffee again. It was getting cold, but it was starting to taste better. I was getting a little jumpy, like I had too much energy. I looked down at the desk where Mother's letter still lay, waiting for me like a promise I hadn't kept. *You are the only one who can tell the truth.* Had they really said that to me, or was it only in the dream? Maybe I made it up.

I picked up Mother's letter. *It's morning here, so you must be in school.* What did she mean by that? Maybe she was just lonely. If all she had to think about was whether we were in school or not at a certain time, maybe she was bored out of her skull. We'd visited her in hospitals before. She always seemed to be making kindergarten stuff—painting wooden plates or embroidering pillowcases, or something domestic like that. She was never domestic when she was home with us. That wasn't really true, though. She tried to be domestic when she was out of the hospital, the way she tried to embroider pillowcases when she was in. She just wasn't very good at it. She wasn't very good at anything. Sometimes she was good at being pretty, but that's not the world's most useful skill. And she could be funny sometimes, but that doesn't put supper on the table, either.

So now she was someplace where she didn't need to make supper, or breakfast, or lunch. Tough turkey . . . *I ate little.*

What would Ron and Diane have said to Mr. Sarow? Would they have backed her up, whatever she said?

No one had told me that coffee does more to you than make you jumpy. I got up and ran for the bathroom, but Diane was inside with the door locked.

"Hurry up, Diane!" I called through the door.

"Hold onto your horses," she said. "I just got in here." I could hear her brushing her teeth and spitting.

"Diane, let me in," I said. "Please—I do it for you sometimes."

"All right, all right," she grumbled. I heard the lock click, and then she opened the door. The toothbrush stuck out of one side of her mouth, and she had toothpaste around the edges.

"Make yourself right at home," she said, as I sat down.

"Don't be so gross," I said.

"Pee-ewe," she said. "You call *me* gross?" She held her nose with one hand and brushed her teeth with the other. Then she rinsed off her mouth, wiped her hands on the towel above the toilet, and turned and unlocked the door.

"Hey, wait a second to open the door," I said.

"I'm all done," she said, and opened the door and walked out. She closed the bathroom door, but it didn't click shut. I grabbed some toilet paper and then scooched over to the door, half crouching, and slammed it shut and locked it.

I washed up, brushed my teeth, and then went back upstairs to look at Mother's letter some more. It seemed to me I had to answer it before she came home on her first home visit, but I didn't know what to say.

Dear Mother, I'm sorry I'm such a wimp. . . .

Dear Mother, I'll never tell another lie again as long as I live. . . .

Dear Mother, I only wanted what was best for you. . . .

Dear Mother, I was afraid for me. . . .

Four crumpled pieces of paper in the wastebasket, and I still couldn't think of a way to begin the letter. I picked up Mother's letter again and read it over. She started out with: *It's morning here, so you must be in school.*

Dear Mother, It's Saturday morning, so you must be painting a wooden plate. . . .

Crumpled paper number five.

Mother's second sentence was about the weather. *The sky is dark now, but it could brighten up.*

Dear Mother, It is a gray day here, and I feel the same way. . . .

Crumpled paper number six.

I pulled out another piece of paper and drew a flower on it with a purple felt-tip pen. I've never been any good at drawing, and it ended up looking sort of like a purple puddle, but at least it took up quite a bit of the top half of the paper. I started again.

Dear Mother,
Today I had my first cup of coffee! Grandma said I wouldn't like it, and I didn't at first, but then I put some milk in it and it wasn't too bad.
We are all fine, but we miss you. Hope we will see you soon. Grandma says you'll be coming home on some home visits.
Love,
Merle

Good thing I hadn't started out by saying I'd never tell another lie as long as I live. What kind of a rotten person would not miss her mother and would not want her to come home from the hospital for a visit?

I took out my purse. Sometimes I had a stamp or two in among the coins, but I must have used them up or lost them; there weren't any stamps in there. As I folded up my wallet, I looked at all the one-dollar bills lined up inside from baby-sitting at the Dvoraks' the night before. What would Mother think if I sent her some money? She might be mad about it, but she probably didn't have any. I wished I had a five-dollar bill; sending a bunch of ones seemed sort of sleazy to me. But a one-dollar bill would hardly be enough even to buy cigarettes.

I walked down the stairs and called out, "Grandma, do you have any money?"

She was just taking her car keys out of her purse, and she looked up at me in surprise. "What kind of a question is that? Do you think they give away groceries at the store these days?"

"I mean, that I could have?"

"I thought you were a baby-sitter now and didn't need anything from anybody."

"Oh, I don't want you to give me money."

"Merle, I don't know what your problem is, but I'm on my way to the store. You should see what Buy-Rite is like on Saturday afternoons. I want to get there before the crowds."

"Do you have a five-dollar bill I could trade for five ones?"

"Why?"

I looked down at the rug. Strands of cream, beige, and lime-green intertwined, like worms beneath my feet.

"I asked you a question, Merle."

"Why does everybody have to ask me questions all the time? Can't anybody ever just take my word for something?"

"What are you talking about?"

I kicked at the rug.

"Merle, you look at me. Right now. Why won't you answer me?"

I opened my purse and took out the five ones. "Here," I said. "Do you have a five, or not?"

She walked over to the dining-room table and set down her purse, her keys, and her fistful of coupons.

She opened her wallet and took out some bills. "I have a ten," she said. "Oh, here's a five." She handed it over to me, and I gave her the ones.

"Thanks a lot, Grandma," I said. "Mother should really—"

"You're sending that to your mother?" she said. "Are you nuts?"

I turned my back on her and started out of the room.

"Merle!" she said. "Listen to me. I never send her cash. I always write her a check. Who knows if they open her mail before she gets it, or what?"

"You send her money?"

"Somebody has to."

"But you—but she—"

"I don't understand you, Merle. Sometimes you act like a grown-up, drinking coffee and going out earning money baby-sitting, and sometimes you act like a two-year-old. Being somebody's mother is a big obligation. I can't just forget about her, any more than I could just forget you kids when she dragged you off to Lake Lune."

"It might have been better if you had forgotten about us."

"I don't think you know what you're talking about, Merle. It could have been dangerous."

"It was dangerous here," I said. "You weren't the only one worried about us, you know. That's why Mother took us away—she was afraid of you."

"All I can say, Merle, is that before you say things

122

like that, you'd better be pretty sure of what you're saying."

"I'm not sure of anything," I said. "All I can see is Mother and that lawyer, both of them telling me to tell the truth."

"What lawyer?" Grandma said.

"Mr. Sarow—at the trial—I mean, the hearing."

"Oh, my God," she said. "Are you still thinking about that?"

"It's pretty hard to forget about it."

"Well, that is the last time I am ever listening to her crazy ideas and drag you kids up to some godforsaken place, where you'll be exposed to all sorts of. . . ."

"Where have I heard that before? You can't protect us from her. She'll get custody back the minute she gets out, and you know it."

"Merle, I can't protect you from much of anything. I can feed you and clothe you and see that you go to school, but I can't protect you from the world. In fact, if you find someone who can, let me know. I could use a little protection myself."

"You're not afraid of anything."

"A lot you know. Everybody's afraid of things, Merle. You're just too young to know that yet. You think because you're a child—"

"I'm not a child—I'm a—a—young adult."

"Fine. But even when you get to be a real adult, you'll still be afraid of things."

"I can't wait."

"You can still get on with your life, whether you're afraid or not. We all make mistakes—I've made some doozies in my life—but you can go on living. That's something I could never make your mother see. She always has thought—and I'm sure she still thinks—that if she runs far enough away, she won't have any problems anymore, or anything to be afraid of."

I looked at her. She had fanned out the coupons and was pulling them from one hand to the other, as though she were dealing cards for a game. She never put them down on the table, though, just moved them from hand to hand.

"But she's sick," I said.

"I know she's sick. You don't need to tell me she's sick. But she never tries, either. If she just tried harder. . . ."

"You don't really believe that, do you?"

"I most certainly do. Your mother has never had a speck of self-discipline in her life. Maybe she could have licked some of her problems if she'd ever set her mind to it, instead of living in a dream world all the time."

"But that's part of her illness, isn't it?"

"God only knows. But I do know that things are going to be different around here when she comes back."

"Maybe she's better off in the hospital."

"You mean, maybe we're better off with her there."

"I didn't say that!"

"No, I said it. But, Merle, she's so miserable there. I just can't tell her she can't come home."

"Do you think money would help? Should I send her this?"

"You do what you want, Merle. But I think it might be better to save it for something special when she comes home the first time."

Grandma stuffed the coupons into her purse, jingled her car keys, and left for the grocery store.

I walked back upstairs with the five-dollar bill in one hand. I kept squeezing it as I walked, as though I could change its shape into something Mother needed or wanted or could use as an excuse to love me again. It was only paper, "legal tender for all debts, public and private." It didn't say anything about imaginary debts, but the back assured me that the government trusts God. It reminded me of a little sign in one of the tacky Lake Lune tourist traps: IN GOD WE TRUST; ALL OTHERS PAY CASH.

That cheered me up a little as I sat down at my desk and stuffed the money into the envelope before I could change my mind.

After school Monday, Diane was sitting at the kitchen table by the time I got home. In her hand was a crumpled white paper covered with purple ditto ink; she was looking at it as though it were a mirror.

"Hi, Di. What's up?"

"Hello, Merle. I don't have any envelopes."

I took the plastic milk jug out of the refrigerator and poured a glass of milk into a Smurf glass. "You want some?"

"No, thanks. How am I going to get thirty-one envelopes?"

"I don't know. Wait and ask Grandma, I guess." I mixed three heaping tablespoons of chocolate-milk powder into the milk. The little blue and white Smurfs looked strange with chocolate milk behind them.

126

"You really like it dark, don't you?"

"Oh, just leave me alone, Diane. I've had a hard day." I sat down at the table across from her.

"Ha! Not as hard as mine." She handed me the dittoed paper.

"What do you need envelopes for?" I asked, as I looked the paper over. "Valentine Post Office," it said at the top. "We live in Doveland, Illinois. Here are our street addresses: Heart Avenue, Flowers Boulevard, Candyland Lane, and Doily Drive." Each "street" had a list of names underneath it. "This is kind of cute, Diane."

"Cute! You wouldn't think so if you had to address thirty-one envelopes by tomorrow morning and you didn't even have any."

"Any what?"

"Envelopes, stupid!"

"I thought Grandma bought some valentines for you. Don't envelopes come with them?"

"Yeah, but they're dinky. We have to have regular-size ones so we can write out the full addresses, with our own names in the corner. Plus zip codes. And there has to be room for a fake stamp in the top right corner."

"Oh, I did that in school once. But it was more like second grade, I think. I don't remember doing it in fourth."

"Whatever. At least you probably had the envelopes."

"I'm sure Grandma has some envelopes in her desk.

127

She uses them for paying all of her bills."

"I'm not going in there, Merle. Not on your life."

"I'll go. You won't have time to do all that writing if you don't start now."

I opened the door to Grandma's room a crack and scooted in sideways. The shades were up, of course—Grandma always opens the shades before she goes to work, even if it's still dark. It's dark again before she gets back home in the winter, but she always pulls the shades up and down every single day. "It doesn't seem right to leave the shades down all day," she said once when I asked her. "But if *you*'re not here, what difference does it make?" I asked. "Well, you kids are here," she said. "At least, you are now. And I have my plants."

I wonder what Grandma did when she was alone in the house when we were in Lake Lune. I wonder if she pulled all the shades up and down, one by one, even though the house was empty from morning till night and she was at work. Weekends were different—then she would have been home during the day. All alone.

Grandma had a few African violets on the windowsills behind the sheer white curtains. The pink, purple, and magenta flowers glowed like little jewels behind a veil. The desk was piled with papers and magazines, bills and stamps, pictures and receipts. Grandma always kept all her receipts so she could claim us as deductions. It was one of the things she and Mother always used to fight about. "*I*'m their mother," Mother would say. Which was true. "But *I* pay the bills," Grandma would say. Which was also true—mostly. Mother paid bills when she was working, but she didn't always work; who knows who paid the most. But the IRS doesn't care who pays what, as long as they get their cut.

The pigeonholes in the desk were stuffed with office supplies—paper, envelopes, reinforcements for paper-punched holes, mailing labels, brown paper, string, glue, and paper clips. Grandma always had to pile the stuff from the desk onto the floor when she paid the bills, but at least she was well prepared.

In one of the pigeonholes there were some small envelopes with blue lines on the front where the address should go. In the upper left-hand corner it said, also in blue: "After five days, return to . . ." with three more blue lines. Grandma had little gummed, return-address labels she put in the corners of bills and letters, but she hadn't put them on these envelopes yet. I figured she must put them on one by one as she used the envelopes. Lucky for Diane.

"Merle!" Diane whispered from the doorway. "Hurry up!"

I jumped a little, and the pile of envelopes fell out of my hand and onto the desk. As I reached to pick them up I saw an enveloped addressed to Grandma. It was a big, business-sized envelope with a postage-meter light red stamp. The return address said: "Department of Mental Health, State of Illinois." I wondered if that meant Mother had been moved to a new hospital. Maybe the letter was even from her. Couldn't be, though; it was typed, and Mother couldn't type two words to save her soul. . . .

"Mental health," I said out loud. "I wonder . . ."

"Merle, just get out of there, okay?" Diane said. "You don't want to be there when Grandma gets home, do you?"

"No. That's for *sure.*"

We left the room and closed the door firmly behind us. "Here you go." I handed Diane the envelopes.

She counted them out slowly, by twos. " . . . eighteen . . . twenty . . . only twenty-one envelopes here, Merle. That's not enough."

"It's plenty for now. Just get started and when Grandma gets home maybe she can find you some more. I don't want to go digging around anymore in her stuff than I already did."

"Yeah, you weren't supposed to be in there."

"Diane, how long have you had that valentine list?"

"I don't know. Awhile. I kept forgetting to bring it home."

"Then quit lecturing me about what I'm supposed to do. Worry about what you're supposed to do—like your homework."

"Okay, okay. You're lucky you're in junior high— you don't have to do valentines anymore."

"Well, you're lucky, too. At least there are envelopes around the house for us to find. Remember when we lived in Westall?"

"No." She sat down at the kitchen table and stared at the fat clump of unaddressed envelopes.

"That was the year I was in first grade."

"I gotta work now." Diane picked up a dull pencil, put her head down almost on the paper, and began to write.

I went into the living room and lay down on the couch. Good old Westall. Lake Lune wasn't the first time we'd gone off to live alone somewhere with Mother. When Grandpa was dying, Mother took us three kids and sneaked off to live in an apartment in Westall. We went there in the middle of the day, while Grandma was at work. Grandpa was already in the hospital by then, so he didn't see us go, either. We just climbed into a taxicab with a bunch of suitcases and pillows and took off for Westall.

Maybe Mother was afraid Grandma would make us come home again or something, but she wouldn't tell her where we'd gone. Which meant Grandma couldn't get hold of her when Grandpa died, and Mother ended up almost missing his funeral. She called one day and Grandma said he'd died and where the hell had she been?

I guess maybe Mother feels guilty that she never said good-bye to Grandpa, but she did go to the funeral. And she goes up to Green Bay to visit his grave whenever she gets the chance.

We moved back to Bronwyn quite a while after the funeral. We must have lived in Westall about a year and a half, because I went to all of first grade and part of second grade there. Ron and Diane were little then —not even in school—but I can still remember Westall. It was sort of like Lake Lune—hardly any furniture, crummy clothes, and cruddy food. Mother never did the dishes until there weren't any clean ones left.

At least in Lake Lune we were old enough to help her with some of that stuff. But in Westall, she took us all to the baby-sitter's in the morning and picked us up just before suppertime. Ron and Diane stayed there all day, and I went off to school with the baby-sitter's kids.

Mother used to get so tired. She would cook supper, but afterward she'd leave all the dishes on the table and lie down on the bed in just her slip and panty hose. Ron and Diane would play, or sometimes they'd go off to sleep then, too. I remember I'd feel lonely. We didn't have a TV for company or a telephone, and I used to write little letters to Grandma on old paper or envelopes Mother had tossed out. Mother always said she'd buy a stamp and mail them to Grandma for me, but I suppose she never did.

When we lived at Grandma's, I always had tablets of paper and a box of color crayons. But Mother never bothered with that kind of stuff—not at Westall, anyway. I suppose she had a lot of problems, but you'd think she could help her own kid make a valentine box.

Serves her right to be locked up in that hospital without even a pencil sharpener. Maybe she can feel what it's like to have nothing—if she even notices.

The night before Valentine's Day in first grade I told Mother after supper that I had to have a valentine box for school the next day. She was already in her slip and she said she was going to lie down for a minute and then I could tell her about it. But she didn't get up again. I kept going in and saying, "Mother, I have to have a valentine box for school," and she kept saying just go to bed. Finally, I said, "Mother, the teacher said an old shoe box would be good. Don't we at least have a shoe box?" She kind of rolled over and said, "Look in the closet," and dozed off again.

In the closet, there were piles of shoes, purses, clothes, paper bags, and, way in the back, a green cardboard shoe box. I opened it up. There wasn't even any tissue paper inside—just some shoes. Then I looked all over the apartment for some scissors and something to cut up to decorate the box with. Finally I found some curved fingernail scissors, but nothing for decorations. I thought of cutting up my doll's dress and using the lace, but I didn't dare. I didn't want to, either. I had seen a little scrap of yellow cloth on the closet floor, so I went back and got that. God knows where it came from; Mother never sewed.

I drew a heart on the yellow cloth and hacked it out with the fingernail scissors. Then I cut a hole in the top of the green shoe box for a slot for the valentines. I couldn't even find any tape, so I sort of punched through the heart and the box with the tip of the scissors to make the two stick together.

The next morning I put the box in a brown grocery

bag. I wouldn't show it to the baby-sitter's kids when they asked to see my valentine box. At school, we had to line up for the Valentine's Day parade first thing. Everyone had their valentine boxes on their desks. Some had little pink hearts on top, or fancy lace doilies, red ribbons, pink streamers, flowers—God knows what covered all the other boxes in the room.

Mrs. Romano came over and asked if I had a box. I took it out of the sack and plunked it down on the desk. There it sat, yellow and green and ugly, like a dog turd. "Well," she said, "I'll bet you made that yourself without any help, didn't you?"

She took my hand and everyone followed us out the door and down the hall. Since we were the first classroom of first graders and I was at the head of the line, I didn't have to see anybody else's boxes. I suppose they saw mine, but I didn't have to see their pink bows.

"Are you sick, Merle?" Grandma asked.

I jumped up off the sofa. The living room was almost dark. "Sick?" I said. "No, I guess I just dozed off or something."

She switched on the big pole lamp and then walked into the kitchen. "Hi, Diane," she said. "You're working hard."

"I'm almost out of envelopes, Grandma. Do you have any more?"

When I walked into the kitchen, Grandma was looking at Diane's writing on the envelopes. "Where did you get these?" she asked.

"Merle went in your room," Diane said. "I told her not to, but . . ."

Grandma looked at me.

"When I got home, she was sitting at the table crying because she couldn't do her homework without envelopes," I said. "What was I supposed to do?"

Grandma shrugged her shoulders and took off her coat. As she turned to go back out to the living room and hang it up in the closet, I asked, "What did the Department of Mental Health have to say?"

Grandma came back into the kitchen. "What do you mean?"

"I saw an envelope—from the Illinois Department of—"

"Probably from your mother."

"No, it was typed."

"They're moving her to Hillpoint, in Illinois."

"Can I read the letter?"

"It is my letter and it's in my room and it's my business."

"But she's my—"

"That is the end of the subject. I'm going to make supper now, so there'll be time for Diane and me to go out to the store and get more envelopes."

"When's she coming home?" Diane asked softly, looking down at her pile of smudgy envelopes. "Bronwyn is in Illinois."

"Duh," Ron said, as he came in the door. "Did you just figure that out?"

"Who said anything about anybody coming home?" Grandma said, shaking out her coat as though it were full of dust. "She has to get well first."

"Mother's in Illinois," Diane said to Ron.

"She has to be somewhere," Ron said. He looked down at the floor and scuffed the toe of his shoe across the linoleum.

"What kind of a crack is that?" Grandma said.

"It's not a crack—it's a scuff mark," Ron said, and then he laughed.

"Sometimes," Grandma said, stirring the chili so hard she mashed the beans. "Sometimes I don't know what's going to happen to you kids."

"Then that makes four of us," Ron said.

I wore red to school the next day—Valentine's Day. It was my red corduroy dress from Lake Lune, the one with the big wooden buttons. I hadn't had it on my body since we'd come back to Bronwyn three months before, and I wasn't as sick of it as I had been then, when I used to wear it every other day.

All the classes were cut short for the annual school talent show. Kayla and I sat together and talked until the lights went down. Jinx came in at the last minute and sat in the empty seat next to me, but she ignored me and leaned across to say hi to Kayla.

The first act was a girl who came out in a long, ruffled prairie skirt with a frilly white blouse; she curtsied to the audience and then sat down at the piano to play. A snicker passed through the audience; curtseying was not cool. She played a short piece called "Rodeo" and then quickly walked off the stage. The long, maroon velvet curtains swished closed.

When they opened again, there was a table in the middle of the stage. A boy in a tall, black top hat and a black coat with tails stood behind the table; to his left was a girl in a swimsuit. This time a loud wave of laughter spread among the kids in the auditorium; then came a few wolf whistles.

"Ladies and gentlemen," said the magician. I looked more closely—it was a guy named Greg I knew from English. "Gregory the Great, assisted by the Magnificent Melanie, will show you some of the greatest magic feats on earth." He stuck out first one foot and then the other and grinned at the audience. A few people groaned, but most everybody laughed. He bowed low, with one hand behind his back and one hand in front. When he straightened up again, the hand that had been behind his back was pulling out a long silk scarf. It was all different colors, a sort of rainbow effect.

"And now, ladies and gentlemen," he said, walking around the stage waving the scarf, "we will see what this scarf can do."

"Nothing!" someone—probably a "plant"—called out from the audience.

"Oh, person of little faith," Greg said, looking pleased. He swished the scarf a little and an egg appeared. He swished the scarf some more and there was a baby chick where the egg had been. *Swish, swish* again

—and there was no baby chick, just an egg again.

"Anyone still wonder which came first—the chicken or the egg?" Greg asked. There were lots of groans this time and no giggles.

"And now, Melanie the Magnificent will disappear!" Greg said. "Right before your very eyes."

Melanie—who was shivering as she stood there on stage wearing very little and doing nothing—stepped forward. She looked as though she were trying to smile, but all of a sudden she fell to the floor.

Greg was busy swishing the rainbow scarf around and his back was turned to Melanie. When he saw what had happened to her, he knelt down and said, "Disappear, Melanie, not faint with fear." He began waving his hands together, as though he were clapping, but didn't quite touch the hands to each other. All of a sudden the maroon curtain swished quickly shut; he must have been signaling to the curtain-puller.

There was dead silence for a few seconds, and then everyone began whispering. A few wiseacres clapped single loud claps with long spaces in between to show what they thought of the act.

After a minute or two the curtain swished open again and we got to sit through about seven more piano players, a couple of acrobats, a baton twirler, a folksinger who sang "Blowin' in the Wind" as though she were making up the words on the spot, and a comedian who laughed at his own jokes. It was almost better to sit in class than sit through that crap.

When the lights came up, Jinx said, "Boy, that girl's future is all behind her."

"What girl?" Kayla said, yawning and stretching out her arms.

"*Mel*anie the Mag*ni*ficent," Jinx said, her voice dripping with sarcasm.

"Maybe you can take her place," Kayla said. "I'll bet you'd be good standing up there."

"That rinky-dink crap?" Jinx said. "Not me." She was holding her arms kind of funny—out a little from her body, but not so far that they'd touch anybody else. She had on a brown long-sleeved leotard, a fuzzy sweater, and jeans.

Her eyepatch was gone; where it had been, her eye was all discolored—green and yellow and purple black. The bruise seemed to be fading, though. That must be some boyfriend she'd found herself.

"Plus you'd have to wear a swimsuit," I said.

She looked at me. "So? I have a swimsuit."

"I didn't say you didn't. But . . ."

"I look a whole lot better in anything than you do, Carlson."

"So?" I said.

"So shut up," she said.

We were having this charming conversation because we were both on our way to fifth-period gym. When we got there, we headed for the lockers, but Ms. Garland stopped Jinx.

"I'd like to see you for a minute, Jennifer."

Jinx kept walking fast, but veered sharply off toward the teacher's office. She didn't look at me or Ms. Garland—just acted like a car steering itself in a different direction.

"How's your eye?" I heard Ms. Garland ask as I went into the locker room. I didn't hear the answer, but anyone could see for themselves that her eye was rotten—sort of like Jinx herself.

I couldn't help thinking about Jinx and her boyfriend, though. Did he get off on beating people up? Was he big and just didn't know his own strength? Or maybe he was little and felt he had to prove himself. Maybe he was just an A-number-one ass. But where could Jinx have linked up with such a creep? And why did she stay with him? Weird.

"Class is so short today that we'll just practice lay-ups," Ms. Garland said, when we were all in the gym. "There isn't time to try to play a real game."

Jinx practiced lay-ups with us, but you could see she was afraid of her eye getting hurt. She'd pull back when she should have kept going; she'd flinch if someone came near her; and she had trouble catching the ball when someone threw it to her because she didn't look at it straight on. Nancy Lieberman had nothing to worry about for the time being.

I walked to sixth-period English with Peggy. There hadn't even been time for showers because the class had been cut so short by the talent show. So we were all sweaty and sticky and we were complaining about it when Maggie Bennett came over to walk with us.

"You think *you*'ve got troubles," she said. "Guess who moved in with us?"

"Another foster kid?" Peggy asked. Maggie's mother took in foster kids. Actually, her whole family took in foster kids, but I think Maggie's mother was the only one who really wanted to do it. Usually they were little kids who would come and then leave again as soon as their parents got it together or whatever. But sometimes they'd get teenagers who'd really raise hell, like the kid who almost burned down their house when he tried to smoke a joint under the covers after everyone had gone to bed.

"No," Maggie said. "Not just another foster kid. Jinx Normandale is not your average foster kid in my book."

Peggy and I stopped walking. "Jinx Normandale?" Peggy said.

"Is living at your house?" I said.

Peggy and I both started to giggle.

"It is not funny," Maggie said. "I'll trade you places any old time. Just try it for a night and see."

"I'm sorry, Maggie," Peggy said. "It's just—of all the people in the world, how did you ever end up with her?"

"Ask me," Maggie said.

"I'm asking," Peggy said.

"I don't know. Ask my mother."

"But what did she do?" I asked. "Why's she in a foster home at all?"

"Would *you* want her, if she were *your* kid?" Peggy asked.

Even if she had lousy taste in boyfriends, it seemed sort of rotten for Jinx's folks to give her away. After all, she was their kid. And blood is thicker than water —whatever that means.

At supper, I asked Grandma if people can just give their kids away.

"What gave you an idea like that?"

"Well, can they?"

"Not exactly."

"Well, how do you get rid of a kid you don't want anymore?"

"I've never looked into it," Grandma said. "Why?"

"There's this kid at school whose parents shipped her off to a foster home."

"How do you know?"

"Well, she used to live with her family, and now she lives with the Bennetts."

"That doesn't prove anything."

"It proves her parents didn't want her."

"Not necessarily. Sometimes kids get taken away from their parents, you know, if the parents are unfit or something."

"Unfit?"

"Well, if they neglect them or abuse them."

"What about if they don't like their boyfriends?"

"Well, I don't know—that doesn't sound too likely to me. Did you see the mail?"

143

"Yeah—there wasn't anything for me."

"On the dining room table, there's something that was slipped into the mail slot. I saw it when I came home from work."

The big, square white envelope was addressed to me. The envelope didn't have a stamp on it or a return address, though. Inside was a construction-paper valentine from Jason. He had carefully drawn a little red fire engine with hearts coming out of a smokestack at the top. Underneath, he had printed in crooked letters: HAPY VALNTIN DAY. MERLE. FROM JASON. On the bottom, Mrs. Dvorak had written, "He's not much of a speller, but his heart's in the right place! See you soon."

What a Valentine's Day—a card from a five-year-old, a stupid talent show, and Grandma had made a heart-shaped red Jell-O mold with cream cheese frosting for dessert. A red-letter day this was not.

16

"I could get used to all *A*'s," Craig Munson whispered to me in homeroom. We'd just compared grades—I got an *A* in English and he got a *B*.

"I don't get all *A*'s," I said.

"You should. Actually, I should, too, but I'm too busy with the *Bronwynnian.*"

"You still the editor?"

He nodded. "When are you going to submit something for us?"

"I don't have anything."

"What about that poem you wrote for Mrs. King's class? The one about trees that she had you read out loud?"

That was how I'd gotten the *A* in English.

"But the *Bronwynnian*'s a newspaper—you don't print poetry, do you?"

"Well, we're thinking of starting a Poetry Page."

"You'll be flooded with entries. Everybody's a poet."

"I know," he said. "That's why we haven't done it yet."

He had his calculator in one hand, and he was flicking his thumb up and down on one of the keys.

"Present!" I said, when the homeroom teacher called my name. Mr. McIntyre called roll every morning. He wanted us to answer loud and clear, but he didn't mind if we talked the rest of the time.

Craig called out "Present!" a minute later. Then he turned to me again. "Well, how about it?"

"The poem?"

"Yeah—what was it called—'Panorama'? You know —the one Mrs. King read out loud a while ago."

" 'perspective,' " I said, just as the bell rang.

"Oh, yeah, 'perspective.' " He stood up and we walked out of the room together. "I don't really care for poetry much."

"Well, thanks a lot!"

"No—that's not what I meant. See, I really don't like poetry at all. . . ."

"You already said that."

He grinned and turned to go down the hallway on the left. I kept walking down the middle corridor.

"Oh, are you going that way, Merle? Wait a sec—I just wanted to tell you that I don't usually like poetry but I liked 'perspective.' Think about it." He waved and walked quickly down the hall, buckling his calculator onto his belt as he walked.

My third-quarter report card had two *A*'s, two *B*'s, and two *C*'s. "This isn't too bad," Grandma said, as she looked it over. "Your mother used to get all *A*'s, though, and I'm sure you could do it, too."

"A lot of good it did her."

"That was before she got sick."

"I know—but it still didn't do her any good."

"It couldn't hurt to work a little harder on your schoolwork, Merle, and I'd like to see you do it."

"Why? What difference does it make?"

She sighed and then wrote, "Mrs. Lillian Ostrand." She dotted the *i*'s with a flourish and crossed the *t* with a dramatic slash before she answered. "Suit yourself, Merle. I can't make you work harder in school."

"I get better grades than my friends. You should see Kayla's report card—she thinks it's cool to get *C*'s and *D*'s."

"Maybe you need some new friends."

"I'll be late if I don't get going."

We had to hand in our report cards in each class so the teacher could be sure they were signed.

"I thought your name was Carlson," Jinx said in gym. I looked up; she was hanging over my shoulder and reading my report card.

I moved away and ignored her.

"Well, isn't your name Carlson?"

"It's none of your business what my name is."

I could hear Jinx whispering to the girls around her. I tapped her elbow, but she ignored me, so I grabbed her arm and squeezed it. When she turned around, I said, "Why don't you just mind your own business?"

She jerked her arm away. "Get your hands off me, Carlson! Don't take it out on me just because you don't have the same last name as your family."

"And I suppose your last name is Bennett now?"

"Bitch!" she hissed, and then she went to sit down on the sidelines.

It was playoff day and we all suited up in our team shirts—everybody but Jinx. She sat on the sidelines and wrote in a little notebook with a spiral wire at the top—probably a slam book, but I couldn't tell for sure.

After a minute I forgot Jinx, though, because our team was getting skunked. We couldn't seem to do anything right. We tripped over each other's feet and missed easy baskets and ran in the wrong direction and lost the ball at the drop of a hat. When the game was over, our side had lost, 57 to 12.

"Good try, girls," Ms. Garland said, as we filed out to go take our showers.

I heard Jinx snicker, but then I ran upstairs and got into the shower before Peggy could.

When I got to home ec., I felt I'd wasted the time I'd spent doing homework the night before. Mrs. Bagg had a whole bunch of stuff written out on the board and we had to copy it all down, word for word, like she'd never heard of a Xerox machine or something.

I was about halfway through when the girl sitting next to me poked my elbow. "Write something and pass it on," she said, handing me a little spiral notebook. The cover was plain red, but the first inside page said: SLAM BOOK. I flipped through. Most of the pages were curled and gray on the edges, but the next-to-the-last page seemed new. At the top, it said: JINX NORMANDALE. I began to read the entries under her name. Each one was in a different color ink, or else pencil. The first page said:

> Kinda stuck-up.
> But what a bod!
> Mouths off too much.
> Why does she always wear long sleeves?
> To cover up the bruises.
> What bruises?
> Her father used to punch her lights out.
> All this hearsay crap makes me sick.

I flipped the notebook over, so I could read the rest of the entries on Jinx:

> Hearsay? Everybody knows that's why
>   she's in a foster home.
> Yeah—her father beat her up all the time.
> Everybody doesn't know that.
> They will now, ha-ha.
> Why doesn't her mother make him stop?
> She took off years ago.

"I'll take that, Merle."
I looked up—Mrs. Bagg was standing right over me.

I quickly closed the slam book and started to put it in my desk.

"I *said* I'll take that, Merle." She reached out her hand and I slowly handed over the little red notebook. How could a little notebook like that be so full of crap?

"I assume this is yours?" she said. She held the slam book tight, but didn't even look at it, just hit it against the palm of her other hand.

"Well, no, I . . ."

Everyone in the class had turned around to stare. Jinx was smirking, and I saw her brush her forefingers against each other and mouth, "Naughty, naughty," behind Mrs. Bagg's back. I wondered if Jinx knew the newest page in the book was about her.

I looked at her long, painted fingernails and her black bangs that almost covered her eyes. It really didn't matter what she thought of me. I wondered what else she was covering up. Was her forehead bruised under her bangs, the way her eye was? Were her nails bruised under her purple nail polish? Could her father really have beaten her up? Where did people hear that story in the first place? Was it a lie?

"Do you know how destructive these—*things*—are, Merle?" Mrs. Bagg asked me after class.

"I never saw it before," I said. "All I did was take it when somebody handed it to me."

"Do you know how much trouble these horrible little books cause? I really am surprised at you, Merle.

150

I thought you had a little more sense."

"Oh, I do."

She looked at me. "Is that why you sat there and read it in my class, while I was explaining how to make an apron?

I started to laugh. I couldn't help myself. An apron, of all things. I laughed until tears came to my eyes. I looked at Mrs. Bagg.

"It isn't very funny, is it?" she said.

"No, I guess not. Do you know what it says about Jinx?"

"Jennifer Normandale has had a good deal of trouble in her life, and I'm not interested in anything that adds to that."

"You mean it's true?"

She stared at me. "I'm not going to report this, Merle. But if I catch you—or anyone else—with a slam book in my class ever again, I will turn him or her over to the principal. Is that clear?"

"Very clear. But why don't the people who start these things around ever get caught?"

"That's one of the mysteries of junior high school. You'd better hurry now."

All through geography I thought about Jinx Normandale and the tiny bit of skin she uncovered to the world. I thought of the day she'd pulled my hair and how surprised I'd been. And then I remembered Jinx's bruise. She didn't get that playing basketball. No wonder she got so upset that day she pulled my hair. She

must have thought I'd seen the bruise—which I did—
and knew where it came from—which I didn't.

"Did you forget your book, Merle?" Mr. Johnson
said.

"No, it's right here," I said, and pulled it out of my
backpack.

"I suggest that you read it, then," he said, and
walked on down the aisle.

*São Paulo is Brazil's most populous state. Its major crops
include coffee, rice, corn, and cotton. It is also an important
industrial region.* Big hairy deal.

After English, Craig Munson asked again if I had
anything for the *Bronwynnian.*

"I'll think about it," I said.

I stopped in the girls' bathroom before my next
class. As usual, the bathroom was full of smoke. There
used to be teachers on "potty patrol" when I was in
seventh grade, but this year they'd decided to put us
all on our "honor." That worked about as well as
outlawing slam books worked, and all the bathrooms
chugged smoke out of their doors during every break
and every lunch hour.

I didn't see Kayla when I walked home from school
that afternoon, and when I called her she wasn't home,
but her mother said she'd have her call me.

She didn't call after supper, though, so finally I
called her again.

"What do you want?" she said, when she came to the

152

phone. I'd heard her telling her mother she didn't want to talk to me.

"I just wanted to say hi."

"Oh—I thought maybe you wanted to apologize."

"For what?"

"That was my s.b. you gave away, you know."

"Your s.b.? What's that?"

"That you gave to the old—to Mrs. Bagg today."

"I didn't give any s.b. to anybody; I don't even know what—oh. Is your mother listening or something?"

"You could say that," Kayla said.

"So it was *your* slam book?"

"Yeah—and I have to tell you I was p.o.'d when I heard you'd let her have it."

"I didn't have any choice—she grabbed it away from me."

"You weren't supposed to let her see you had it, dummy."

"I didn't do it on purpose."

"Oh, don't be such a scuz, Merle." In the background, I could hear her saying something to her mother.

"You should talk—I thought you were a friend of Jinx's."

"So what?"

"So why'd you put her name on the last page of your slam book?"

"What's it to you?"

"It's not the kind of thing a friend should do."

153

"Thanks for the tip."

"Kayla, did you read what it said about her?"

"Some of it. I passed it around this morning, though, and somebody was stupid enough to give it to you, and now I'll never see it again."

"But how can you say you're a friend of Jinx's? What kind of a friend would—"

"I've never heard you say two good words about Normandale—what's it to you?"

"But I didn't know. . . . Is it true?"

"Who cares? It's just a stupid slam book. Hers only had a couple of entries when I passed it on this morning. It's not supposed to be the God's truth or anything."

Kayla's mother must have left the room.

"Kayla, did Jinx do something to you?"

"No . . . why?"

"I can't figure out why you put her name in then. I thought you liked her."

"She's okay. But now that she's living with the Bennetts, she'll never be able to go anywhere or do anything. . . ."

"You can still be friends in school, can't you?"

"Oh, Merle, don't be such a nerd. A friend is someone you hang out with. The only place I'll see Jinx now is in the can at school, sneaking a smoke."

"You are something else, Kayla."

"Better believe it. See ya, Merle."

When the *Bronwynnian* came out Friday, I looked for the Poetry Corner but there wasn't one. But on the back page—the sports page—there was a huge drawing of a basketball next to a column of type. HIGH JINKS, it said at the top, BY JENNIFER NORMANDALE.

The High Jinks column wasn't especially well written, but it was definitely thorough. Everything that had anything at all to do with basketball—no matter how remote—was in that column. Even the details of our 57 to 12 playoff score in gym class. Jinx must have been taking notes in that little notebook during the game.

"Not bad, huh?" Craig Munson asked, when he saw me reading Jinx's column.

"Did she write this all herself?"

"Well, I cleaned it up a little, but . . ."

155

"Huh."

"Deadline for next week is Monday. Why don't you bring that poem in? We've got a couple of others now, so I think we'll start the Poetry Corner."

Over the weekend, I copied "perspective" over so I wouldn't have to give Craig my only copy. And when the *Bronwynnian* printed it on Friday, I really liked the looks of it:

"perspective"

>gray trees
>enveloped in mist
>lights twinkle through
>the branches—
>pliable prison bars—
>allowing only glimpses
>of the night
>   —m. g. carlson

"Looks good, M. G." Craig said, when I saw him in English. "What's the *G* stand for?"

"Glenda."

"Glenda? Sounds like a witch."

"It does not—it was my great-grandmother's name."

"Oh. Do you have anything for next week?"

"I'll check."

Over the weekend I worked on "lavender." Craig called Sunday night. "I had a hard time tracking you down, Merle. Do you know how many Carlsons there are in the Chicago phone book?"

"No, how many are there?"

"A lot. And I didn't even know your father's name."

"So how'd you find it?" I thought of my father, living God knows where. No one had to look him up under *my* name.

"I called Jim Billings. He's on the *Bronwynnian,* too. He mentioned one time that he went to elementary school with you."

"He would. I suppose he told you about the time I was a crossing guard and just about knocked some kid's teeth out with the flag?"

"No. I'd love to hear about it sometime, though. Sounds dramatic."

"Not from me."

"But right now I wanted to know if you'd written anything for this week's Poetry Corner?"

"Well, yeah, I did. It's called 'lavender.' "

"Why don't you read it to me? We could always change the title."

"Thanks a lot." It didn't take long to read the poem:

"lavender"

        i can't think
        of looming
        black lilacs
        i only see lavender
        pretty and pale

When I'd finished, Craig didn't say anything for a minute. Then he said, "That's it?"

"Yeah—what do you think?"

"Forget it, M. G. No poem with the word 'pretty' in it will run in the *Bronwynnian* as long as *I'm* the editor."

So that was the end of my literary career for a while. But Jinx's kept right on. Every week, there was the big basketball with Jinx's by-line and the title: HIGH JINKS. People even started calling her High Jinks, which she didn't seem to mind.

Ms. Garland decided to organize an after-school basketball league. Kayla thought it was completely scuzzy. As she put it, "Who wants to run around and sweat with a bunch of wet armpits when you could be having pizza with some guys at McGrew's?"

Kayla was not improving with age, it seemed to me, but I did agree with her on one thing—no way was I going to stay after school and play basketball, either, even though I didn't go with her to McGrew's.

The star of the new league, of course, was old High Jinks herself. There were even pictures of her in the *Bronwynnian* from time to time—Jinx jumping up to make a basket, Jinx dribbling, Jinx taking notes at the game. What with Jinx writing the basketball column and referring to herself as "Yours Truly," as in "Yours Truly made the last basket, in the final seconds of the game," and her picture being in the paper all the time, there were a lot of people who thought something was kind of fishy. I noticed, though, that in the pictures, anyway, Jinx was wearing more regular clothes—short-sleeved shirts with no turtlenecks underneath, shorts with white socks instead of tights. Her eyepatch was long gone and she'd even trimmed her bangs some—maybe so she could see the ball better.

The other big change in Jinx's life was that she'd found a boyfriend, Bruce Ramette. He was the photographer for the *Bronwynnian*—that was part of why people thought the "High Jinks" column was kind of fishy. Did she get her picture in all the time because she was so good, or because Bruce wanted to take pictures of her?

Jinx and Bruce made a fairly strange-looking couple. They'd walk around the halls with their arms around each other, Bruce's camera and camera bag and extra rolls of film and extra lenses bumping into their hips, chests, arms—wherever the equipment happened to be, it would bump them. They were too absorbed in each other to notice. They practically made out in the halls, which grossed a lot of people out.

I was walking to class with Maggie Bennett one day when Jinx and Bruce walked by, looking at each other as though the map of the school were in their eyes.

Maggie clicked her tongue and looked the other way. "I don't believe it," she said.

"What?"

"Oh—nothing. It's just that my mom has told her and told her—"

159

"Told her what?"

"To cool it with that guy."

"Why? He seems to make Jinx pretty happy. She's in a lot better mood than she used to be."

"Ha!" Maggie said. "Ha-ha!"

"You don't like Bruce, either?" Maggie had a boyfriend, too, so I didn't think she'd be jealous. She and Dylan used to have a crush on each other even in elementary school. I thought it was a little strange to pick out a boyfriend in fifth grade, but then, at least she had a boyfriend.

"What's there to like?" Maggie said.

"I don't know. I suppose he must have something going for him, or what would Jinx see in him?"

"That's a good question—I don't have a clue."

I forgot about Jinx and Bruce and the *Bronwynnian* when I got home, though. I'd gone to the library after school to work on a research project for geography, and when I got home Grandma was talking on the phone.

"How long a visit?" I heard her say. "You think she can handle a whole weekend?"

I hung up my coat. "Well, if that's what the doctors feel is best," Grandma said. "You want us to come get her Friday? I work, you know. Would Saturday morning work out? Otherwise, the bus. . . ."

"Okay, we'll be there Saturday morning.

"Oh, boy," she said, after she'd hung up the phone. "Give me strength, is all I can say."

"For what? Is that about Mother?"

"Yes, that's about *Mother*," she said.

"Oh."

She sat down in the rocking chair and slowly began to rock back and forth. Her arms were crossed over her chest, as though she were cradling a baby or a doll.

"Is she coming home or something?"

Grandma didn't answer me, just rocked back and forth, back and forth, and stared at the rug.

"Well? Is she?"

She looked up. "Yes, she's coming home for the weekend. If all goes well, she'll come for a couple more weekends, then for a trial home stay. If that works out, she'll be home for good."

"For good. Right."

Grandma stopped rocking. "We'd better get supper started and then go get her room ready. I don't think there are even any sheets on her bed. I stripped the beds after you took off for Lake Lune, but she hasn't been back. . . ."

We put blue-flowered sheets on Mother's bed and plumped up the pillows and spread out the bedspread and tossed the two throw pillows on top. Mother's room seemed dusty and smoky; some long-ago cigarette smoke still hung in the air, but it was like the smoke of a ghost. It was creepy being in her room when she wasn't there; I wasn't all that fond of that room when she was there, in fact.

I wondered what she'd be like when she came home. I sort of wanted to be there, and I sort of wished I could be an angel hovering invisibly above when she came home. Then I would hear her and see her, but she wouldn't be able to see me or say anything to me.

After supper, Grandma came upstairs to help us kids make our beds fresh, too. "Might as well change all the beds at once while I'm at it," she said, stripping the quilt off my bed and draping it over a chair. The part on top said GLENDA AND KARL in wrinkled letters.

"Were your parents happy?" I asked Grandma.

"What kind of a question is that?"

"I just wondered—they made that quilt together, and everything. . . ."

"Ha! If you think Papa ever lifted a finger to help Mama do anything, you have another think coming. He had his work and she had her work."

She turned her back and started out toward Diane's bed.

"But they had all those kids—don't you think they were a little bit happy?"

"You have a lot to learn," Grandma said, as she picked up some pink-striped sheets for Diane's bed.

I picked up the quilt and waved it across the bed, then straightened the corners. Usually I put it on the bed plaid side up, so that the crazy-quilt side wouldn't get worn out. I flipped it over and spread it out over the bed with the other side up for once.

Glenda and Karl. First husband and wife, then mother and father, then grandparents and great-grandparents, and on and on forever—even after they were dead they were somebody's relatives. They'd be my kids' great-great-grandparents. And they'd hardly

162

ever even met me, let alone my kids. Over and over again, new couples, new names, new kids. All different shapes, all different sizes, but all part of the same family, all linked together by blood.

How could a father hit his own kids? Did he hit their mother, too? How could someone hit his own daughter hard enough to leave a bruise?

Might as well ask: How could someone kick her own daughter? Of course, Mother wasn't a child, like Jinx. She was old enough to defend herself. She could always leave.

That's what Mother had done—she'd left for Lake Lune to defend herself. But it didn't work. She was running away from her problems—maybe Grandma was right.

Or—maybe both Mother and Grandma were wrong. How could I decide? What did I know? That lawyer should never have asked me that question. I should never have been in that courtroom. There must have been two dozen adults in that courtroom in Muskeegoom—and they had to call in a thirteen-year-old girl to help them decide what to do. What they should have done was so clear—Mother needed to get well.

They didn't need me to tell them that. Maybe they never planned to listen to what I said, anyway—maybe it was all Mother's idea and didn't make a damn bit of difference to anyone.

Anyone but me and Mother. Even if she held it against me forever, how could I have said something that I thought would get her out of the hospital when she wasn't well?

Someday I'd have my own kids and my own husband and my own family. Someday I'd get to decide how things were done, and it wouldn't have to do with kicking or punching. And I wouldn't marry someone who'd desert me like my father or Jinx's mother—people who see a rotten situation and just leave so their own life can be better, who forget about their kids and leave them in a place they couldn't stand to stay in.

If you build something good for your kids, it's a better life for you, too. If Mother and Grandma had thought more about us kids and less about themselves, maybe their own lives wouldn't have been so terrible.

The ride down to get Mother on Saturday morning wasn't very long—only about an hour—and everyone was in a pretty good mood, considering. None of us knew what we were going to say to Mother, but on the other hand, there was no point in worrying about it, because what we said to Mother was going to depend on what she said to us, anyway, and God only knew what she was going to be in the mood to say.

We didn't go inside the hospital with Grandma, but just waited outside in the car. We looked at the big, old, yellow brick buildings with the bars on the windows. The grounds were beautiful, with big trees beginning to leaf out and patches of bright green grass. I wasn't sorry we didn't go inside. That day we'd spent in the courthouse in Muskeegoom had sort of cured me of my curiosity about big government buildings.

After a long time, Mother and Grandma came out together. Grandma had brought some clothes for Mother and she was wearing those, so thank God she didn't come out in her Lake Lune chino pants and plaid shirt. That would have been too much to take. Her hair was combed very nicely, all sort of puffed up and curled, as if someone had done it for her at the hospital. She even had makeup on; she looked pretty nice.

Ron got into the backseat with Diane and me when we saw them coming.

"Hello, kids," Mother said, as she got into the front seat. She leaned over and gave each one of us a quick peck on the cheek and a quick, stiff smile. I waited for some torrent of words, but she was quiet the whole way home.

After being in the house with just Grandma for six months or so, it seemed very strange to have Mother there again. I was nervous about what she would do and say, but she didn't do or say much at all.

As soon as we got home, Mother headed for the rocking chair. She sat down hard in it, *clunk*, put her purse on her lap, and lit up a cigarette. She just rocked and smoked, and smoked and rocked, and sat there like a lump.

None of us really knew what to say, so we all sat quietly in the living room, too, except for Grandma, who went into the kitchen and made lunch.

"Well," Mother said, finally. "It sure is good to be home."

We all said stuff like, good, sure, I'll bet, and then there was another long silence.

"You miss me?" Mother said, looking at me.

I looked down at the green rug and rubbed my shoe into it. "Of course we missed you, Mother," I finally said.

"Well, I wondered," she said.

Mr. Sarow and the courtroom flashed onto my eyeballs. Jesus Christ, would I have to look at that the rest of my life, right in there with my Lake Lune slides?

I decided to see what she was driving at and hear it once and for all. "Why wouldn't we miss you?"

"Well, you didn't write very often. The mail was all I had to look forward to, you know."

That was promising—anybody's mother can be upset about not getting enough letters.

"Merle's been too busy baby-sitting," Diane said.

"I wondered where you got the money," Mother said. "Who were you baby-sitting for?"

"Jason Dvorak. The same as before we—" I stopped and looked at her.

"The same as before we—" she said, sweet as pie. "Before we what, dear?"

My God, had they given her shock treatments again? Did she remember Lake Lune, or didn't she? If she didn't remember Lake Lune, she wouldn't remember Mr. Sarow, either.

"The same people I used to baby-sit for before," I

said. "Mrs. Dvorak was supposed to have a new baby by now, but she . . . doesn't."

"Why not?" Diane asked.

"It died," I said.

"It died?" Mother said. "How did it die?"

"Well, it didn't exactly die—she had a miscarriage."

"We've all got troubles," Mother said. "Did you miss me?"

We started in with sure, you bet, of course, again, until finally Grandma called out that lunch was ready.

Mother stood up stiffly from the rocking chair and held her purse in front of her. She walked slowly and jerkily into the kitchen, clutching her purse to her chest. I heard Grandma say, "Why don't you put your purse down? Nobody's going to steal it; we're all friends here."

Mother sat at her old place at the table, with her purse on her lap and her hands folded on top of it.

"Hey, where am I supposed to sit?" Ron said.

We all looked down at the four plates on the table. Grandma looked surprised and quickly turned around to get another plate from the cupboard.

"Go get another chair from the dining room, will you, Ron?" she said. She put the plate down on the table and carefully turned it around until the stem of the rosebud in the middle was down and the flower up. Diane and I moved plates around until they were all equidistant. Ron kept his mouth shut for once, even though we all knew he liked where Mother was sitting, right by the window.

Mother didn't say a word, just looked at us as though we were performing some dance she didn't know.

Grandma opened the silverware drawer and took out a knife, fork, and soupspoon from Mother's silver-plate pattern and not her own stainless steel. We kept all the flatware in the same drawer, but they argued about which to use all the time. Grandma would say stainless steel is practical and doesn't show water-marks; Mother would say silver is beautiful. Of course, the silver was wearing off the backs of the silver-plated spoons, but that sort of thing never bothers Mother. For her, it's the thought that counts, and silver is silver, whether it's coming off or not.

We ate vegetable soup, crackers with butter, milk, carrots, and celery. The coffee was perking away in the aluminum pot on the stove, and when it was done, Grandma took out two mugs. "Care for some coffee, Elaine?"

"Thanks much," Mother said, jerking her head strangely as she reached to take the mug. She added milk and then took a sip. "Good coffee."

"Maybe I'll have some, too," I said.

As I reached into the cupboard for a mug, Mother said, "Since when are you drinking coffee?"

"Since a while ago. I told you in my letter. I'm almost fourteen now, you know."

"I know the date better than anyone," Mother said. "I was there."

"So was I."

Everybody laughed and relaxed a little.

"I was hoping I'd be back for good by Merle's birthday," Mother said to Grandma.

"That's not up to me," Grandma said.

"Oh, I think it is," Mother said, in the meaningful tone she sometimes uses to make statements that don't mean anything at all.

"Where'd you get an idea like that, Elaine? I'm not your doctor."

"You'd like to be. You'd like to tell me what to do, and where to go, and what to say, and how to say it."

"Don't you start that again," Grandma said. "I'm not listening to that kind of talk in my own home."

Mother looked down at her purse. She began rubbing the brown vinyl with her fingers, round and round and round, as though she were polishing it.

I took a sip of the coffee and then spat it back into the mug. "Hot!" I said.

Mother looked up. "I told you you were too young."

"I'll let it cool down a little." I put the mug down.

"As I recall, Elaine, you were drinking coffee at about her age."

Mother looked back down at her purse. "I hoped Merle would be more sensible than I was."

"*That* wouldn't be hard," Grandma said.

"I guess not," Mother said. "If you don't want that, Merle, I could use a little more coffee."

"There's more on the stove," I said, and took a tiny sip.

"Did you hear what I said? I *am* your mother, after all."

"You think you can just come in here and snap your fingers and be my mother all over again?"

She gave me a look like I was the one who had a screw loose. "What are you talking about? I'll always be your mother."

"Yeah, but it's not the same now," I said.

She opened her purse, took out a cigarette and some matches, and lit up.

"Why are you fighting already?" Diane asked.

"We're not fighting," Mother said. "We're having a discussion. At least, I'm trying to." She licked her forefinger and rubbed the side of her purse again.

"I've started drinking coffee and I'm going to keep on," I said.

"They used to say it would stunt your growth," Grandma said.

"Remember how Grandma Nana used to give us kids sugar lumps to dunk in the coffee, Mother?" Mother said.

"I sure do," Grandma said. "Everybody slurping at once."

"Sounds like a bunch of horses," Ron said. "Sugar lumps?"

"We'd each have a doll-sized teacup," Mother said.

"No, they were demitasse cups," Grandma said.

"Whatever. Little cups, anyway, filled with coffee and milk. And we'd get two sugar lumps each."

"Your father used to tease Mama until she'd give

171

him a couple of sugar lumps, too," Grandma said.

"Daddy always had a sweet tooth," Mother said, drawing in on her cigarette.

"Speaking of a sweet tooth," Grandma said, "I made brownies." She brought out an aluminum cake pan with a clear plastic lid; she must have made a double batch.

While she was passing brownies around and Diane was clearing the table, I kept thinking, *He's not dead, he's just sleeping. He's not dead, he's just sleeping.* I wondered if Mother still thought that, or if she'd gone back to regular thinking for a while. Just because she wasn't saying it didn't mean she wasn't thinking it—that was for sure.

After we'd finished lunch the phone rang. Ron raced to get it. "For you, Merle!" he yelled. "It's Kayla!"

"Merle, can you come over?" she said, after I said hello.

"Uh, I don't think so."

"Please? I really need to talk to you."

Out of the corner of my eye, I saw Mother walking into the living room. She sat down in the rocking chair and lit up a cigarette.

"Kayla, we have company," I whispered into the phone.

"What? I can't hear you."

"We have *company*; I can't come over today."

"Please, Merle? Just for a few minutes? I really need you to."

"Well, I'll try, Kayla. I'll call you back if I can't."

When I hung up the phone, I turned around. There sat Mother, rocking and smoking and looking at me.

"Company, Merle? Who exactly is this company we have?"

"Oh, Mother, it was just Kayla. It doesn't matter what I say to her."

"Or what you say about me, apparently."

"Well, but she sounded so . . ."

"I really do not care how she sounded. I am your mother, and I say you cannot go over there this afternoon."

Grandma came in then. "Go where this afternoon?"

"I'll handle this, Mother. It's between me and my daughter." She ran her fingers through her hair, as if she were trying to get it to come down farther over her face. It wouldn't budge, though; just got a little ratty looking.

"What'll I say to Kayla?" I said. "How can I explain?"

"Don't say anything," Mother said, "except that you can't go over there."

"It's easy for you to say that. She's not your friend."

"You've hardly mentioned her all winter," Grandma said. "I don't see why you should be so keen on seeing her the very day your mother comes home on a visit."

"I'm not a visitor," Mother said. "I live here."

Grandma looked at her, but didn't say anything.

"Where my children are is my home," Mother said.

"Poor Jinx," I said. I wondered if her father felt the same way about her, no matter what he did to her.

Mother stared at me. "What did you say? That I'm a jinx?"

"No! See, there's this girl at school whose nickname is Jinx, and . . ."

"I never heard of this Jinx person before," Mother said.

"She's the Bennetts' foster child—remember Maggie Bennett?"

"Why wouldn't I remember Maggie Bennett?"

"It was just an expression. Anyway, Jinx and Kayla are like this." I crossed two fingers on my right hand and held them up. "Or at least they were before Kayla's slam book."

"What's a slam book?"

"It's too complicated to explain right now. I have to get over to Kayla's before she thinks I'm not coming."

"You're not," Mother said. "You're my daughter. I need you at home." She lit up another cigarette and then shook the fire out of the match.

"You have two other children," Grandma said. "I don't see any harm in Merle's going to see Kayla for a few minutes. You could talk to Ron and Diane for a while."

"Why don't you stay out of this?" Mother said. "This is my private conversation with Merle."

"This is my living room," Grandma said. "I see you're making yourself right at home."

"Why shouldn't I?" Mother said. "It's my home, too."

They hardly noticed when I slipped out the door and ran over to Kayla's. They were busy getting back to their favorite indoor sport—fighting.

"Glad you came, Merle," Kayla said, when I rang her doorbell. She looked really strange, with makeup so thick I could hardly see her skin. Her hair was combed far down over her face. She had on a big, white, man's dress shirt, about ten sizes too big for her, with the sleeves rolled up. Plus tights with sandals over them.

"So what's the big deal, Kayla?"

"I need your help, Merle. Jinx ran away."

"From the Bennetts'?"

"Yeah—they said she couldn't see Bruce anymore so she split." Kayla pulled me inside the house and closed and locked the door. "My parents are gone for the weekend, and I'm supposed to be staying at somebody else's house. But when Jinx called, I told her she could stay here last night, anyway. But now I don't know what to do."

"What about the people where you're supposed to be staying?"

"Oh, I called and made up some excuse. They're cool. But Jinx can't stay here forever, so we were thinking . . ."

"Jinx is here? Right now?"

"At this very moment," said a voice behind me. I turned around, and there stood Jinx. She looked like Kayla on the outside—makeup, hair, tights, sandals, white shirt—only with Jinx underneath.

"How ya doin', Jinx?" I said, with a little phony smile; always the lady. I felt like the Scarsdale Diet doctor's mistress. Here are some flowers. How're you doing? *Bang, bang.*

"Never been better in my life, Carlson. What'd ya think?" Jinx shook her head so that her bangs brushed her eyebrows.

"So who else is coming?" I asked Kayla. "This is quite a little party you have here."

"No, that was last night," Kayla said and giggled a little. "That's why we look a little wiped out. But there's some tequila left—you want any?"

"Where'd you get that?" I asked.

"Oh, here and there," Kayla said vaguely. "Everybody brought something and we made fisherman's punch—God, was that awful."

Jinx said, "My dad calls it fish-house punch, but his tastes better than that stuff last night."

"Anyway, you want some tequila, Merle?" Kayla said impatiently, glancing at the clock on the table.

"I don't think so—I can't stay very long. Is there something special you wanted to tell me, or . . ."

"We like you so much, we thought we'd invite you over to hang around," Jinx said.

"But my mother's just home for the . . . weekend."

Jinx stared at me. "Bull."

"No, it's true. She's been . . . sick."

"Again?" Kayla said.

I sat down on the couch. "Yeah, again."

"Jesus, Merle, that's too bad."

"So little Goody Two-Shoes Merle's got problems, too," Jinx said. "Well, tan my hide."

I stood up. "Did you invite me over to start that crap again? Because if you did, I'm leaving."

"No," Kayla said. "We invited you over to see if you want to join the WBs."

"You did?" I said in a squeaky voice. I cleared my throat. "You did?"

"Well, don't wet your pants, Carlson," Jinx said. "It's not that big a deal."

I smelled a rat. "Why do you want me to join, anyway?"

"Well, when you didn't say anything about whose slam book it was, we figured maybe you were okay, after all," Kayla said, but she didn't look at me.

"Nobody asked me whose slam book it was."

"You could have told, anyway."

"Why would I?"

"Some people are just born mean," Jinx said.

She should know, I thought, but I didn't say it. I

thought of Mother and Mr. Sarow. *Only you can tell the truth, Merle. Only you can tell the truth, Merle.* I wished I could just pluck that slide out of my memory carousel and stuff it into the garbage.

"Jinx needs to buy a bus ticket, Merle," Kayla said. "And she can't really go buy it herself—somebody might see her. She's going to take a really early bus tomorrow morning."

"You want me to go downtown and buy Jinx a bus ticket? This afternoon?"

"Yeah."

"Why don't you ask somebody who was at your party last night?"

"They're all too wiped out," Kayla said, "and most of them are grounded from here to kingdom come to boot." She giggled a little and looked very pleased with herself, but then looked a little worried. "I just hope to hell they have the sense not to tell where the party was."

"But why should *I* help you?" I asked.

"We'll let you be in the WBs if you do."

I thought of the trick we used to play as kids. *Here, let me pull out your chair for you.* And then we'd pull it so far back the person would sit down on air and fall to the floor.

"I'll bet," I said.

"No, I really mean it," Kayla said. "Cross my heart and hope to die if I should tell another lie."

"Where's the bus ticket to?" I asked.

"Hyde Park," Kayla said.

179

"Why do you want to go there? Do you have enough money to live on?"

"She knows somebody in Hyde Park," Kayla said.

"My old man lives there," Jinx said at the same time. "I can crash with him."

"But I thought your father . . ." Kayla said.

Nobody said anything for a minute.

"Jinx, why do you want to live with your father?" I asked.

She glared at me. "That's a stupid question, Carlson. Why does anybody want to live with their father?"

"Everybody's father doesn't beat them up," I said. "I saw that bruise."

She jumped on me before I even saw her start to move. She slammed her fist into my side as hard as she could, twice. I thought I was going to faint.

"Cut it out!" Kayla yelled. "She'll never help us if you beat her up, Jinx." Kayla pulled her away.

"I'll never help you, period," I said. "Jinx, you are a genuine, honest-to-God born moron. What's the matter with you, anyway? You're going to leave a perfectly good foster home . . ."

"They're creeps," Jinx said, shaking her hair.

"I know the Bennetts—they're not creeps."

"How would you know? You're a creep, too."

"Probably everybody's a creep," I said. "But not everybody beats on their kids."

"Carlson, you have diarrhea of the mouth," Jinx said. "If you're not going to help us out, why don't you just go home. We'll think of something else."

"I don't know . . ." Kayla said. Somebody must have told her what had been in the slam book, after all. "I didn't know you were going to your father's. . . ."

"You thought maybe I'd go to my *mother*'s?" Jinx said sarcastically.

Kayla and I stared at each other. Finally Kayla cleared her throat and looked over at Jinx.

"Look, Jinx," Kayla said. "Maybe Merle's right. Maybe you should go back to the Bennetts' house."

"And be grounded for a month? They are *steamed* about Bruce."

"Why?" I said. "He seems like a pretty nice guy to me."

"Well, we had a . . . fight," Jinx said. "And he—uh —sort of—slapped me around a little."

"A little!" Kayla said. "Show her your stomach!"

"Forget it," Jinx said. "I've got on about five layers of clothes."

"He hit you?" I said.

"Well, I mean, I sort of hit him a little, too," Jinx said. "But the Bennetts got on their high horse and said no foster child of theirs was going to be allowed to go out with someone like that—that any guy that would hit me wasn't good enough for me. As though I were their frigging real daughter or something."

"Makes sense to me," I said.

"I'll bet," Jinx said. "No one's asking you, anyway, so you can have all the ideas about guys you want. At least Bruce asks me out."

"I'd rather stay home," I said.

"You *would*," Jinx said. "But not me. I like to go out. And if the Bennetts ground me for a month, I won't have a friend left."

I thought of Grandma's comment that maybe I needed some new friends; Jinx could use a few, too.

Kayla was staring at her sandals.

"I'm not going back to the Bennetts'," Jinx said. "I can buy my own damn bus ticket—I don't need you, Carlson."

"We can be friends even if you're grounded," Kayla said.

Jinx looked at her. "How?"

"Well, we could probably talk on the phone sometimes. The Bennetts would let you do that, wouldn't they?"

"I don't know," Jinx said. "And I'm not going to ask, either."

"Why not?" I said.

"Will you butt out, Carlson?" Jinx said.

"But how are you going to know what they're planning if you don't ask them?"

"People never tell you what they're really thinking, anyway," Jinx said. "What's the point of asking a bunch of questions when the answers don't mean anything?"

"Some people aren't like that," I said. "Some people mean what they say."

"You make me sick," she said. "No matter what you're doing, you act as though it's the right way to do it. Even if you make a fool of yourself playing basketball, you act as though you couldn't care less."

"I do?"

"Did you ever read what Kayla's slam book said about you?"

"No, I didn't get a chance."

"Luckily," Jinx said. "Everybody thinks you're Miss Priss."

"Well, everybody who writes in slam books, anyway. That doesn't include the entire world, you know."

"See, that's what I mean," Jinx said. "Whatever you do is perfect. Whatever anybody else does is stupid."

"If you read what Kayla's slam book said about you, you might change your mind about people who write in slam books."

"I wasn't in Kayla's slam book—I read the whole thing."

"Yes, you were—on the very last page. It was the newest one."

Jinx turned to Kayla. "Why'd you put me in there?"

Kayla looked nervous. "It was just a stupid slam book. No big deal."

"But the WBs were supposed to write about other people, not about each other."

"It's no big deal," Kayla said again.

"Well, shit," Jinx said. "Maybe Maggie Bennett was right about the WBs."

"What'd she say?" Kayla asked.

"That you were all a bunch of mental midgets and

you'd stab me in the back as fast as anyone." I noticed she said "you" about the WBs and not "we."

"That's Maggie's opinion—she's always been a nerd," Kayla said.

Jinx didn't answer, just stared at a spot on the wall next to Kayla's shadow.

"I have to go," I said. I walked toward the door.

"I guess I will go home," Jinx said, to no one in particular. "I mean, back to the Bennetts'."

"Well, see ya," I said, and walked out.

As I closed the door, I could hear Kayla saying, "I'll help you get your stuff together, Jinx." And in the background I could hear the words to "Personal" on the radio:

> Straight white male of twenty-one
> Wants a girl who's full of fun.
> No strings allowed; I don't want no ties—
> Just a good-time girl with laughing eyes.

When I got home, I could hear Ye Olde Family Fight even before I opened the door.

20

"Greetings," I said, as I walked in.

" 'Bout time, Merle," Ron said. "You sure do know how to pick a fight."

"Come off it," I said. "I wasn't even here."

"No, you left as soon as you'd started it," Ron said. "They've been yelling ever since."

"That's just too bad," I said. I started walking toward the stairway.

"Merle, you stay here with us," Mother said. "You've been gone all afternoon as it is."

"I've been gone an hour, and I'm not listening to any more fighting today."

"Merle's too good for the rest of us," Grandma said. "Didn't you know, Elaine? Of course, you haven't been here to see it, but all she does lately is sleep and throw her weight around, now that she's a *poet*."

She said *poet* as though it were a dirty word.

"Or thinks she is," Ron said. "*I can't think of looming black lilacs . . .*" he recited dramatically.

I kept walking.

"Merle!" Mother said. "Answer your grandmother."

"She didn't ask me a question." I kept walking, but more slowly.

"Merle, turn around," Mother said. "Don't you leave this room."

"What is it?" I said.

"I'm only home for the weekend, Merle. Come and talk to me."

"In a while, Mother. When everything's calmed down a little."

I started to walk toward the stairs again.

"If you go upstairs now," Grandma said, "you can just plan on skipping supper tonight."

"Fine." I put my hand on the door to the staircase.

"All the time I put into raising you," Mother said bitterly. "I would have been better off raising dogs or cats."

"That was your decision," I said. "No one forced you to get pregnant."

Grandma started to laugh. "It's starting all over again," she said. "Pretty soon she'll be telling you she didn't ask to be born, Elaine!" She laughed and laughed. I turned around and looked at all four of them, but I absolutely could not think of anything to say.

"Snap out of it, Merle," Ron said. He snapped his fingers a couple of times.

"Will you grow up, Ron," I said, and walked upstairs.

I closed the door to my room, kicked off my shoes, and stretched out on the bed. The quilt was spread out crazy-quilt side up, so it was a little bumpy, but I didn't feel like flipping it over. I looked around the room. The deep blue-green walls were darker than the pine tree outside the window. The sunset was making the room a very peculiar color: a combination of greens, blues, oranges, and reds. Iridescent would almost be the word for it, only it didn't shimmer.

After a while, the doorknob turned and the door opened. I looked over, and there stood Mother, purse in one hand, ashtray in the other.

"You *could* knock."

"I want to talk to you, Merle."

"Be my guest." I gestured toward the desk chair, but it was covered with clothes and books.

"I'll just sit down here," she said, sitting on the edge of the bed.

"So what do you want to talk about?" I asked, as she lit a cigarette.

"There's something I want to know, Merle."

"I'm sorry about what I said to Mr. Sarow, Mother."

"Mr. Sarow? Oh, you mean the lawyer. What you didn't say, you mean."

"Yeah."

"Well, that's all water under the dam, or over the bridge, or something, now. I'm getting better."

I could hardly believe my ears. If she thought she was getting better, she must think she used to be worse.

I stood up and walked over to switch on the overhead light. "Let's just sit here and watch the sunset," she said.

"It's awfully dark, Mother."

"We don't need it to be very light just to talk."

"What do you want to talk about?"

"Something's been bothering me. . . . I keep thinking about it."

"I *told* you I was sorry about Mr. Sarow. What more can I say?"

"Not about that. We don't have to talk about that."

I stood up and walked over to my desk and switched on the small lamp. Then I took the top blouse off the pile on the desk chair and began to button it up. *Button, button, who's got the button. Got a button loose? Got a screw loose? Button your lip. Button the blouse. What are we going to buy it with, buttons?*

"You don't have to do that now," Mother said.

"No. But I want to."

She sighed and lit another cigarette. She looked around the room, then sighed again. "Do you have to do that now, Merle? Couldn't you just turn the light out again and come sit by me? We're not going to have much chance to talk before I leave tomorrow."

I put the blouse back down on the chair and

switched the light out. Then I walked over to the bed and groped my way to the far side. I crawled along where the bed hit the wall. Then I sat up cross-legged, my hands on my ankles.

Mother puffed on her cigarette; the glow lit up her face until it was the color of the sunset just passed. I heard her inhale the smoke deep into her lungs and hold it there. One, two, three, four, five, six. . . . God, she must have an extra lung or something to hold it that long.

Suddenly she exhaled and coughed. "I hope I'll be coming home soon."

"Yeah, me, too." I reached down and felt the top of the quilt. When I found one of the little nubs of yellow yarn, I worked it between my fingers and a little of it began to stick up. I twirled that little strand around and around between my thumb and four fingers.

"I've missed you," she said. "All three of you."

"We've missed you, too, Mother."

"It's awful there. Oh, Merle, you just don't know. . . ."

I don't want to know, either, I thought, but I didn't tell her that. I just said, "I suppose it must be."

"You're so young. Thirteen is so young."

"I'm almost fourteen."

"I know. Do you like any special boys?"

"Not right now."

"That Ricky in Lake Lune was a good-looking boy. We had some good times there, anyway, didn't we?" She inhaled on her cigarette again and held it. Her face in the glow looked young and puffy, almost like a child's face. How could she think we'd had fun in Lake Lune?

"Lake Lune was a dump, and Ricky was a jerk."

"A dump? You call that beautiful lake a dump?"

"I wasn't thinking so much of the lake."

"You'd think of the lake plenty if you'd been where I've been. I think about the lake all the time, the way it sparkled in the sun."

I tugged harder on the little yellow yarn. How could I stand to listen to this? She was going to break my heart; how could I help her? All of a sudden the yarn broke and my elbow shot backward, into Mother.

"What did you do that for?" she yelled. She jumped up. "Oh, God."

I got up, too. "What's wrong?"

"Turn on the light, quick."

"I thought you liked the dark."

"Will you turn on the damn light?"

I scrambled around her for the light switch. "What's going on?" I said, when I could see her in the light. She was on her hands and knees, looking for something on the floor. I thought of her "washing the floor" with a torn T-shirt that last night in Lake Lune.

"Help me, Merle! Quick!"

"Help you do what?" I stared at the floor but I couldn't see anything. After a second, though, I smelled something.

"Oh, my God, Mother, did you drop your cigarette?"

"Yes, thanks to you."

"It wasn't my idea to sit in the dark." But I got down on the floor, too, and looked for the cigarette.

"Well, it was your idea to hit me. I don't see why you elbowed me like that."

"I didn't do it on purpose. It's just that the yarn in the quilt snapped. . . . Oh, my God, the quilt."

I crawled out from under the bed as fast as I could and stood up. I looked at the quilt. There, right in the center, was the cigarette smoldering in the fabric.

"There it is!" I reached for it, but there was nothing to pick up; it had burned almost to a cinder.

"Smother it!" Mother yelled.

"You smother it! I'm going to go get some water!" I ran to the bathroom, but the door was locked, so I ran down to the kitchen. Grandma stood at the sink peeling potatoes. I grabbed a mixing bowl from the cupboard. "Excuse me, Grandma."

"What's your big hurry, Merle?"

"Uh, nothing much." I turned the water on full force and it splattered over both of us.

"Will you watch what you're doing?" she said. "What's the rush, anyway?"

"Uh, nothing." I turned the water down and prayed it would fill fast.

"Hurry, Merle!" Mother yelled from upstairs.

Grandma looked at me. "What's going on?"

"Uh . . ."

"Hurry, Merle!" Mother yelled again. Her voice sounded closer this time.

191

"Go back upstairs and watch it," I yelled back.

"Watch what?" Grandma said.

I grabbed the bowl and ran with it. It sloshed as I ran, so I had to slow down to a fast walk. By the time I got halfway up the stairs, I could hear that Grandma was following me. When I got into my room, I stopped a minute to find the exact spot of the smoldering. Then I carefully poured the entire bowl of water onto the center of the quilt.

"Are you crazy?" Grandma said from the doorway. "That quilt is an heirloom. You'll ruin it pouring water on it like that."

"Fire'll ruin it worse," I said. I went back downstairs to get some towels to sop up some of the water.

"Fire?" I heard Grandma say. "Fire? What's this about a fire, Elaine?"

"Nothing," Mother said. "Just a little misunderstanding, that's all."

When I came back with the towels, Grandma was sitting on the bed, looking at the wet spot in the middle of the quilt. Mother stood stiffly over by the window, her elbow crooked to hold her purse.

I put the folded towels down over the wet spot. "Not like that," Grandma said. "You have to unfold them so they can blot it up."

I unfolded the towels and laid them down, one over the other, on the quilt. "I'm sorry, Grandma," I said. She didn't answer me, just stared at the towels. "I'm sorry," I said louder. "I didn't mean to do it."

"Nobody means to do anything around here," she said. "Everything's just a big damn joke."

I leaned over the towels and sort of scrubbed them back and forth, trying to get them to sop up the water, so I could look to see if there was a burn mark.

"Stop that!" Grandma pushed my hands away. "You'll ruin it."

I let go of the towels and sat down with my back against the wall, facing her.

"Mama made that quilt. She worked on it the whole first year she was married."

"It's beautiful," I said.

"She used to sew all the time—with so many kids, she had to. But she always said this was the best quilt she'd ever made."

I looked over at Mother, who was still staring at the window; the black night reflected her own face back at her. But then I realized that, standing at the angle she was, she probably could see Grandma's face better than her own. She was watching Grandma to see what she was going to do; she was afraid.

"How did this happen?" Grandma asked.

Mother stared at the window glass.

"It was my fault," I said.

"You don't smoke."

"No, but, see, it really was my fault, because . . ."

"Stop making excuses for her! It couldn't possibly have been your fault. You think the entire world revolves around you, but it doesn't."

I reached over and pulled the towels aside. There was a huge, wet circle right in the middle of the quilt. The burn mark was about two inches long and an inch wide. It went all the way through the cotton batting in the middle and the gray-and-blue plaid; I could see the blue-flowered sheet underneath.

Grandma was staring at the burn mark, too. "Mama's quilt," she said. "And it's Mama's name that got burned."

Sure enough—AND KARL was there with the date all intact, but GLENDA was gone, except for a few tufts of embroidery floss here and there.

I heard Mother click open her purse and take out a cigarette. She struck a match and lit up.

"Haven't you caused enough trouble with your *everlasting* cigarettes?" Grandma said.

"Nothing lasts forever," Mother said.

"You can certainly say that again," Grandma said, and laughed a weird, little laugh.

"It can't be the first time anything ever happened to . . . it," I said. "In all these years."

"That's right, make excuses," Grandma said. "What's an old quilt to you, anyway?"

"Why did you put it on my bed if it's so valuable?"

"Mama gave it to me, her oldest daughter. And since you're named after her, I wanted you to have it." She looked first at Mother and then at me. "I thought it would mean something to you."

"It does."

"I doubt it." Grandma started smoothing out the quilt, stretching it just a little with her fingers to see how it looked spread out. "If you cared about it, you'd take care of it."

"Maybe I could patch it."

"We don't have the fabric anymore. It's too late."

"We could add a new patch—after all, the whole thing is patchwork."

"We'll have to do something," Grandma said. "We can't just leave it like this."

Mother walked slowly across the room, her cigarette in one hand, the ashtray in the other, her purse over one arm. She didn't look at us, and she didn't say anything. She walked jerkily toward the door, as though it took all her concentration to do that.

"Elaine," Grandma said. "You can't smoke in the bedrooms. I won't have it."

Mother sucked deeply on the cigarette, then ground it out in the red plastic ashtray. "Okay," she said. "I won't." She held the ashtray in front of her with both hands, as though it held water that might spill.

"You want to finish peeling the potatoes?" Grandma asked. "I think Merle and I had better take a look at this quilt."

Mother pivoted around. "What potatoes?"

"The ones in the sink in the kitchen. I've got them started, and the peeler's on the drainboard."

"Peel the potatoes," Mother said, and then she laughed a little. "I wonder if I remember how."

"Practice makes perfect," Grandma said pointedly.

"They use instant at the hos—" Mother said. "Instant potatoes taste like mashed cardboard."

"Then riced potatoes should taste good to you tonight," Grandma said. "And I bought pork chops."

"Pork chops," Mother said. "With bones in them?"

"That's how they grow," I said. "Oink, oink."

"Not in institutions," Mother said. "They grind them up and then roll them out like cookies or something. Everybody calls it mystery meat."

"No mystery about these," Grandma said. "They were on sale, but even so, with the price of pork what it is, we can only afford pork chops for special occasions."

"Is this a special occasion?" Mother asked.

Grandma got up and walked over toward her. I looked down at the sopping wet towels on the quilt. When I looked up again, Mother had lain one hand stiffly on Grandma's shoulder and Grandma had one hand on Mother's cheek. "It's good to have you home, Elaine," Grandma said. She gave her a little kiss.

"Oh, Mother." Mother looked down at her shoes. Her shoulders slumped down around her bowed head.

Grandma smoothed her hand over Mother's hair and tucked a stray wisp back into place. "You'd better get those potatoes peeled if we're going to have any supper."

Mother walked slowly down the stairs.

"My mama made this quilt while she was pregnant the first time," Grandma said, as she sat down on the edge of the bed. She twirled some of the stray bits of yarn and threads around as though she could reweave them with her fingers. Then she poked her forefinger into the cotton batting in the middle. I could see the outline of her finger moving around inside the quilt, feeling for the shredded parts.

She flipped a corner of the quilt from front to back, studying how it was put together. "These old quilts started out as patches," Grandma said. "In the old days they just used whatever they had on hand and made up the design as the went along. I guess there's no reason we can't do that to mend it."

21

We ended up cutting a circle out of some gold velvet Grandma had in her ragbag. I embroidered around it with blanket stitches, using thread in the same gold color. Then we ironed iron-on interfacing onto the back of that, then pieced some gray flannel onto the back side. Grandma found some embroidery floss just about the same color as the original black—although the old floss had faded—and I embroidered GLENDA where Grandma wrote it with a pen.

"Well, my handwriting's different from Mama's," Grandma said, as she looked it over when we were done. "And your stitches are about twice as big as hers, Merle." She stepped back to look at it some more. "But from a distance I'd say hardly anyone would ever know the difference."

Mother was back in the hospital by then, but I

wrote to her about the quilt. I told her it looked "good as new," which wasn't quite true. It looked different than new—but no point in worrying her. And there wasn't anything she could do about it, anyway. She couldn't sew or anything. But I could sew for her—I was glad Grandma hadn't had to patch the burn mark herself. It made things easier for all of us.

I even got a poem out of the quilt:

quilting

i wanted my quilt to be perfect
i chose the colors with care
i picked out a pattern to follow
it would be lovely, but rare.

my pattern had called for bright colors,
but the patches got dingy and gray.
the reds clashed with the purples
and black got in there some way.

when my quilt was finally finished
i studied it slowly, with pain
where had my pattern gone?
had all of my work been in vain?

i looked my crazy quilt over
my planned pattern was not there at all
but each piece of the quilt was sewed flat
in its own place, still and small.

—m. g. carlson

199

"Yeah, we'll print this," Craig Munson said, when I showed it to him. "You've got some good images there."

"You sound like a teacher!"

He looked embarrassed. "Well, at least you got the *pretty* words out of there!"

Later, he asked me if I'd edit the Poetry Corner next year. "I've got Jennifer Normandale lined up to edit the whole Sports Page next year, not just do her column, and if you'll take over the Poetry Corner, my job will be a lot easier."

"I don't know, Craig. Jinx and I aren't exactly best friends."

"You don't have to be best friends to work on a newspaper together, for pete's sake," he said. "All you need for that is to both speak English."

"I always wanted to work on the school newspaper," Mother said, when I told her about it on her next home visit. "But I never did."

"Why not?"

"Well, there was this girl who hated me—remember that awful Melody Smith, Mother?" she said, raising her voice so Grandma could hear.

"The one who was so rich?" Grandma said from the kitchen. "Yeah—what about her?"

"I was just telling Merle that she was on the school paper, so that's why I never was."

"You let her keep you off?" I said.

"I just didn't like to be around her," Mother said. "She couldn't have kept me off the paper if I'd decided to be on it, I guess, but it didn't seem worth the bother."

All of a sudden she smiled at me, one of her old, warm, beautiful smiles, like the sun coming out in the winter. "But I'm glad you're going to be on the paper, dear. You're lucky you didn't have to deal with Melody Smith."

"I guess so."

I told Mrs. Auerbach about it when we next went to see her. The Mental Health Department finally came through with family counseling for us when Mother was about to be discharged. This Mrs. Auerbach was okay, even though she wasn't a brain trust. She understood some things really well, like when she said, "Some people deal with stress by avoiding conflict." But she seemed awfully dense about others.

I showed her "quilting" when it was published in the *Bronwynnian*. "Very nice," she said. "But I wonder . . ." She paused for a long time.

"Yeah?"

"Do you notice anything a little unusual about this poem?"

"No."

"About the spelling, or . . ."

"The spelling?"

"It's very interesting how you've spelled all the *i*'s and your name lowercase."

201

"I spelled all the everythings lowercase."

"That's true. I still think it says something, though."

"Like what?"

"Well, something about the way you see yourself."

I told Mother about that when she came for her next home visit. "Well, so capitalize the letters," she said.

"But that's not the point."

"I wouldn't worry about it if I were you. She probably doesn't know too much about poetry, anyway."

"No—I guess not. Did I tell you Mrs. Dvorak's pregnant again?"

"That's nice. That reminds me of the question I never got to ask you last time."

This time we had the lights on and I was working on some counted cross-stitch instead of fiddling with the quilt. If you've got nervous fingers, you might as well keep them busy.

"Yeah?" I said, counting eight threads to where the next stitch began.

"Did your . . . did you ever get your . . . have you started? . . ."

"No speeka the English?" I looked up at Mother; she smiled back at me.

"Did your granny come again yet?" she asked, and then quickly looked out toward the window.

"My granny! Since when did you start calling her granny?"

"Merle, don't ask stupid questions. You know what I mean"—she lowered her voice—"the curse!"

"Oh, you mean my period. Yeah, that started again a long time ago."

"I was so worried about you, honey, and you never mentioned it. . . ."

"Well, I didn't know you were worried about it, Mother, or I'd have. . . ."

"Why wouldn't I worry about my own daughter?"

"Well, it's just that sometimes you get sort of preoccupied. . . ."

"Sweetheart, where you're concerned. . . ." She didn't finish her sentence. "I love you all so much," she finally said. "Sometimes I can hardly stand it for missing you." She opened her purse and took out a pack of gum. "Want a stick?"

"No, thanks."

"It's Juicy Fruit."

"Have you quit smoking or something?"

"I'm trying to. One of my doctors thinks. . . ." She looked embarrassed.

"You can tell me about your doctors, Mother—I don't mind. I told you about Mrs. Auerbach."

"I know. But what would Daddy think if he saw me in a . . . hospital?"

"Oh, Mother, he'd want you to get well."

"He'd be ashamed. You never knew him—I know he'd be ashamed of me."

"I don't think so, Mother."

"How do you know?"

"He loved you, didn't he?"

She drew back as though I'd slapped her. "Of course

he loved me. No one ever loved me the way he did. He adored me—and I ran away without saying good-bye."

I could feel tears brimming over in my eyes. If only Mother could cry, maybe she'd feel better. I put my sewing down; I couldn't see to count.

"Don't cry, Merle. I don't think I can stand it if you do."

I blinked my eyes a few times until the tears went away. My throat still hurt from the tear swelling, but Mother couldn't see that. It was a good thing I was getting grown-up, because Mother never would be; I could see that now. Even when I was six and needed a valentine box she'd let me down, and all the other times since then. But as long ago as junior high she'd been backing away from situations she couldn't deal with; that was before I was ever even born.

Mother came for home visits from time to time. The weekends when she was home, Grandma stayed home, too. But the other weekends, she'd go out with Jack. I couldn't figure out if she didn't want Jack to meet Mother, or if she didn't want to leave Mother home alone with us kids, or what, but Mother never did meet Jack.

Sometimes Jack would come for supper during the week, and he did things with Ron every once in a while—father-son–type things. At supper one time he asked how Mother was doing.

"She's getting better," Grandma said. "Anyone want more potatoes?"

"Any news on when she'll be coming home for good, Lily? I'm getting anxious to make plans."

Grandma looked down at her plate.

"This isn't the time to discuss it, Jack. It's a big decision and a big change for me."

"What is?" Diane asked.

"Yeah, what are you talking about?" Ron said.

"I hope to be your grandfather pretty soon," Jack said, then clapped his hand over his mouth like a kid who's spilled the beans.

"You do?" Diane said.

"Really, Jack, I don't think this is a good time to . . ." Grandma said.

"Oh, hell, Lily," Jack said. "They might as well get used to the idea. When their mother is back on her feet again and we've tied the knot . . ."

"You're getting married?" I said.

"We're talking about it," Grandma said.

"Name the date," Jack said.

"Jack, I don't think we should get the children all excited. . . ."

Grandma had made an apple pie and we were chowing it down when Jack said, "She *is* getting better, isn't she?"

"Who?" Grandma said. "Would you care for a slice of cheddar?"

"Their mother."

"Well, yes, as far as I know."

"I don't see the problem, then. We can help her get on her feet financially and find them an apartment."

Ron and Diane and I looked at each other out of the corners of our eyes. *Now what?*

206

Grandma didn't say anything.

"She's a grown woman, Lily. She has to take responsibility for her own . . ."

"I've tried to explain to you that it's not as easy as it sounds, Jack. She isn't just sick for a while and then well for a while. She kind of fades back and forth. . . ."

"Well, all I can say is she's got you wrapped around her little finger."

Jack looked mad. I'd never seen him mad before, but he really looked pissed. He looked like he wanted to pound his fist on the table, but instead he looked pleadingly over at Grandma.

"I can't decide tonight, Jack. I have to think it over." She stood up. "You kids get the dishes done. I'm going to walk Jack to the car."

They walked through the living room and put on their jackets. "Good night!" Jack called, as they left the house.

We had all the dishes done, the kitchen floor swept, and the counters wiped off by the time Grandma came back inside. She closed the door quietly, hung up her coat, and sat down loudly in the recliner. I heard the footrest open out.

"Did Jack go?" I asked.

"Time for bed, Merle," she said.

"That's really neat about Jack," I said.

"He bought me a ring," she said.

"Let me see!"

"I didn't accept it." She leaned back and closed her eyes.

"Why not? What did it look like?"

"It was a pearl with little diamonds around it."

"And you gave it back?"

"You can't take a ring if you're not going to get married."

"You're not? But why? He's such a nice guy. . . ."

"Nobody's perfect," she said. "Besides, he doesn't have any idea what he'd be getting into."

"Well, it would help if you introduced him to Mother."

She opened her eyes. "Your mother is not the problem."

"What is, then?"

"You kids. He's raised his family and he thinks Elaine should raise hers."

"Maybe that's true."

"I can't just abandon you three, Merle. You need me."

"Well, we're getting sort of grown-up, Grandma. At least I am."

"I can't just leave you to the mercies of whatever hair-brained scheme your mother might come up with next. It's not right. I have an obligation here."

"But you should be able to get married if you want to."

"There are lots of things I want to do, Merle. And I can't do all of them."

"Like what?"

"Well, I might want to go on a cruise to the Caribbean, but I can't very well leave you kids alone here while I'm gone."

"That's different."

"I don't think it is. Jack's pretty close to retirement age and he's always wanted to travel. No matter what he says now, I don't think he'd go for the idea of taking all of you along with us on trips. And once we were married, what could I say?"

"But we could stay with Mother when she's better."

"You've seen how that turns out, Merle. I could never forgive myself if something happened to you kids. Nothing is worth taking that risk."

"What did Jack say when you told him?"

"He thinks I'll change my mind. Lots of women have wanted to marry him since he got divorced, and I'm the first one he's asked. He can't believe I'm turning him down."

"I can't believe it, either."

"I tried to explain it to you."

I dreamed that night that I was all alone in a room full of masks. Then people appeared behind the masks. There were two kinds of masks—Mother masks and Grandma masks. I had to guess which one of the hundreds of masks hid my real mother and my real grandmother. If I didn't guess right, I would lose both of them. And the weird thing was that either one of them could have been behind either mask. It was like there were no rules. And all the masked people were laughing at me. *Choose me. Or me. Or—tee-hee—me.* They were

209

mocking me. *Who do you think you are? We're the only ones who count. You must spend all of your life looking behind masks for us. You will never solve the riddle of who we are. And until you do, you will never be happy. And when you do, you will never be happy.*

When I woke up, Diane was leaning over me, saying, "What is it, Merle? What's wrong?"

"Huh?"

"Why were you screaming?"

I sat up and rubbed my eyes. "I had a horrible dream," I said. "Just horrible."

"What was it about?" she said. She sat down on the edge of my bed and put her hand on my shoulder.

"It was about Mother and Grandma and I couldn't find them and everybody looked like them but they weren't there."

"Ick," she said. "No wonder you got scared."

"Well, we'd better go back to sleep, Di. Thanks for coming in."

She reached over and kissed my cheek. "Merlie, it'll be okay," she said. Then I heard her bare feet padding softly back to her own bed.

When morning came I felt better about the dream. In the daylight, it didn't seem quite so scary, but it still seemed strange.

Craig Munson asked me in school whether I'd have something for the next Poetry Corner or not. I said I thought I would.

"I'm going to write up a weird dream I had."

"Just don't make it *pretty*," he said.

"Don't worry about that. It wasn't a pretty dream. It was really kind of scary."

"Sounds good. We need some scary stuff."

"Not this scary."

"Hey, High Jinks!" Craig called as Jinx Normandale walked by. "You make it to that hockey game Friday night?"

"I sure did," she said. "The story's in the story box. I can't go this week, though."

"What? We're losing our star writer?"

"Why don't you send Carlson? She can write."

"Not sports," I said.

"You don't have to be good at sports to write about them," Jinx said.

"Well, I qualify for the first part, anyway," I said. Jinx and I grinned at each other.

"What is this, an in joke?" Craig asked.

"Sort of," Jinx said. "Well, I gotta go."

We watched her walk away. "I don't know how to *score* a hockey game, even," I told Craig, as she walked away.

He looked at me. "Well, I'll just have to go with you and explain the rules."

"Sounds great. Where is it and how do we get there?"

"In Rochelle, and we take the team bus. Maybe we can get a pizza first or something."

"Okay."

"And get that poem in by Monday."

"I have to write it first."

"Shouldn't take you long—you don't even have to capitalize the letters or anything."

"I'm going to stop doing that."

"Why? It's distinctive."

"I'll find some other way to be distinctive. Someone said not capitalizing *i* makes it look like . . ."

"Like what?"

"Like I don't like myself very much."

"What a pile . . ."

"Or that I don't take myself seriously or something."

"Just when people know who m. g. carlson is, too."

"I'll still keep using my initials."

"That's something, anyway. Although Merle's a pretty name."

"*Pretty?*"

Craig laughed. "Sometimes it slips out. Where'd your folks get a name like Merle, anyway?"

"I don't know. It means blackbird, but I don't think they knew that. Maybe they did."

"Well, at least they didn't give you 'Glenda' as a first name. I can just imagine what that means."

"It was my great-grandmother's name. I suppose they picked it because of that, not because of what it meant."

"And not for its beauty."

"I guess she was called Glennie for short—she probably hated it, too."

"Say, listen, Merle, you know the Eighth Grade Dance?"

"Yeah?"

"Would you like to go?"

"As a reporter?"

"No, as a girl—I mean, together—with me."

We both giggled a little.

"Sure," I said. "Why not?"

"We're doubling with my brother."

"Oh—it'll be nice to meet your brother."

"He's looking forward to meeting you, too."

"How'd you know I'd say yes?"

"I didn't. But I told him I'd ask you."

"How does he know who I am?"

"Well, I talk about you sometimes." Craig looked embarrassed.

"You do?"

"And I, uh, showed him some of your poems."

"And he doesn't like poetry, either, right?"

"No, he hates it!" Craig laughed. "But I'm sure he'll like you."

We were in the *Bronwynnian* room. There was an old cloakroom that the staff used to store things like paper and rulers and old issues of the paper. There was no one in either room.

"I've been meaning to ask if you have any extra copies of the issues with my poems in them."

"Let's go see."

We walked into the cloakroom and Craig kicked the door shut with his foot. It was pitch-dark as soon as the

213

the door closed, though, so we groped around for a light switch. Our hands brushed against each other and when the lights came on we were practically touching.

"I'm sure we have extras," Craig said. "Probably over . . ." He turned toward me and put both his arms around me; then he kissed my cheek.

"I really like you, Merle."

"Ummmm," was all I could say; my mouth was against his shirt.

He squeezed harder and then let me go a little. I smiled up at him. "I like you, too, Craig."

We heard a noise in the outer room; someone must have come in.

"Now, where are those back issues of the *Bronwynnian*," Craig was saying, his back to me, as Mrs. King walked in.

"They're not over here," I said. "Oh, hi, Mrs. King."

"Things are a little disorganized back here, aren't they?" she said. She looked from one of us to the other and smiled a little, as though she knew a secret.

That night I dreamed of a pile of fabric scraps. There were pieces of the material from my chino pants at Lake Lune, and the tacky plaid shirt I'd worn there. There were pieces of a red corduroy dress and a green sweater, blue gym shorts and blue team shirts. There were pieces of green velvet I'd never seen before, polyester plaid I never wanted to see again, and gold from the center we'd sewn on the quilt. There were all colors—red, blue, green, yellow, orange, purple—everything. They were in weird shapes—sharp and pointed like broken glass ornaments, round circles, a heart shape cut with dull scissors, a funny-looking star, rectangular white envelopes, bells, trees, diamonds. They were all in a pile like pieces of a jigsaw puzzle.

All those different pieces—different shapes, different sizes, different colors, different edges—came together slowly in the dream to form a crazy quilt like the one Great-grandma Glenda had made so many years ago. But it was a different quilt, with different colors and different fabrics. Right in the center it said: MERLE AND . . . somebody and a date, but I couldn't read it.

A quilt never starts as one piece, but, in the dream, by the end there was a beautiful quilt made into a whole—pieced out by what was broken or spoiled. The edges were smoothed, stray ends sewn down. And the quilt lay flat and smooth, ready to warm and ready to please.

Jocelyn Riley was born in Minneapolis, Minnesota, and received a B.A. in English from Carleton College. She has published work in *The Boston Globe*, *The Bulletin of the Society for Children's Book Writers*, *The Christian Science Monitor*, *Contemporary Literary Criticism*, and *The Writer*. Ms. Riley lives in Madison, Wisconsin, and is currently president of the Madison Professional Chapter of Women in Communications, Inc.